THE ULTIMATE EXPERIENCE

WE ARE NO LONGER LETTING FEAR HOLD US BACK!!!

THE ULTIMATE EXPERIENCE

WRITTEN BY
MORGAN LINSON

Copyright © 2023 Morgan Linson

All Rights Reserved. No part of this book may be reproduced, stored in a retrieval system, or transmitted, in any form of by any means, electronic, mechanical, photocopying, recording, or otherwise, without the written prior permission of the author.

Hardcover ISBN: 979-8-9883335-4-8
Paperback ISBN: 979-8-9883335-2-4
EBOOK ISBN: 979-8-9883335-1-7

Dedication

My book is dedicated to anyone who has a passion and deep burning desire to travel but has allowed fear to hold you back from your *Ultimate Experience*. Even to those who are already fellow travelers, I hope you find enjoyment in this book. Our time here on earth is short enough…. So let's take advantage and maximize our experience while we can.

Acknowledgment

To family, friends, and mentors who guided me in my career to fulfill my dream to travel the world. Lastly, to my grandmother and guardian angel, Willie Mae Terry aka "MOMO". She raised me up and provided me a foundational structure that I could build upon, and I am grateful to her. Forever and always in my heart.

About the Author

Be inspired and inspire others to change the narrative of how our stories are written.   *–**Morgan Linson***

Morgan Linson is a Registered Nurse, College Professor, and Licensed Real Estate Agent. She is the founder and CEO of a non-profit organization by the name of Mor Girls with Goals. In addition to her organization, she is the owner of Mor Life, which is a travel accessory company.

    Being a nurse is not just her profession. It has been her life's dream. Nursing opened doors for Morgan's second passion, traveling the world. It has afforded Morgan flexibility and financial freedom. But more than anything, it gives her profound satisfaction to make a difference in the lives of the patients and family members she cares for.

Her love and dedication to nursing was so tremendous that she took it a step further. Morgan began teaching nursing at a local community college, which she also attended after high school for classes. Now, she is known as 'Professor Linson'. Never in a million years did Morgan think that she would be teaching nursing! To her surprise, it has been gratifying knowing that she is providing a solid foundation for all her students and ultimately contributing to making a difference in the future of healthcare.

Morgan's journey in nursing began at the age of 16. She dedicated herself to an extracurricular program at George Washington Preparatory High school, for students who wanted to become Certified Nursing Attendants. At 17 years old, Morgan finished the program and started working at a convalescent home after graduating high school. Once in the role of a Certified Nursing Attendant, Morgan quickly realized she wanted to help patients even more. It motivated and drove her to pursue becoming a Registered Nurse.

The aspiring nurse learned that many appalling healthcare disparities existed for minorities. Issues such as higher rates of illness, injury, disability, mortality, access to treatment, and quality of care, to name a few. These disparities inspired Morgan to make a positive impact on her community. She would accomplish this by seeking higher education in order to adequately advocate and inform patients about not only their disease, but how to manage it beyond the hospital setting in order to obtain optimal health.

To date, Morgan has worked tirelessly for 16 years for the County of Los Angeles, serving and treating patients regardless of their inability to pay. She's found great reward and gratification in her endeavors.

Thousands of patients and four college degrees later, Morgan Linson—a health care provider, is proud of the path she chose.

In addition to nursing, Morgan earned her real estate license to become a skilled investor and spread awareness about the importance of ownership, especially within the black community. Becoming a homeowner at an early age was one of her greatest achievements, and the best financial decisions she's made thus far. Home ownership to Morgan means liberation and freedom. Eventually, she'll explore the real estate market as an agent (of course, whenever she can find the time.)

Mor Girls with Goals is a non-profit organization founded by Morgan. Its dedicated mission is to teach girls and young women how to love themselves, understand who they are, learn who they are becoming, decide what they want out of life, and go after it early in order to get a head start. In-depth, Mor Girls with Goals is rooted in the belief that all girls have infinite potential, and that their socio-economic status should not stifle it. Morgan's focus for her organization is to continue to promote education, to provide financial literacy, career readiness, exposure to international travel, expand horizons, create life experiences that will leave a lasting positive impression, and promote mental

& physical health. In her experience, it is easier to prevent than it is to cure, and it is more effective to build strong girls than it is to repair broken women. Youth mentorship is a necessary and vital component of Morgan's organization.

Mor Life is in an arena of entrepreneurship that is new to her. Morgan always says she is more of a working woman than a boss. However, she wanted to challenge herself to do something different, which is business. Everything about travel is what Mor Life exudes. Being that Morgan loves to be comfortable, confident, organized, and safe on all her journeys… everything sold from her brand is travel accessories that provide just that. Mor Life provides items such as packing cubes to organize your luggage, satin-lined hoodies and caps to preserve your hair from sweating out, memory foam neck pillows for sleeping upright on the plane, compression socks to prevent leg swelling and clot formations during long flights, passport covers to keep your travel documents safe, and more. Morgan didn't want to start just any business; She wanted to provide quality products that would truly add value to travelers. Visit www.morlife.shop to purchase all of your travel accessories.

Amidst everything she encounters in her daily life—nursing, teaching, being a CEO and business owner, traveling has been Morgan's source of sanity and relaxation. It is the reward that she provides herself for working hard and always doing her best. Having visited nearly 70 countries and 5 continents, her perspective on life and respect for other cultures, religions, and ethnicities has broadened significantly. Her love for travel influenced and guided her to write this book. Morgan's mission is to be inspired and inspire others to change the narrative of how our stories are written. To help people without agendas. To advocate and protect. To be amongst innovative leaders moving the community and culture forward toward positive change for the future.

Contents

Dedication — v

Acknowledgment — vii

About the Author — ix

Introduction — 1

Chapter 1: The World to Explore — 5

Chapter 2: Starting from the Basics — 19

Chapter 3: Get Ready — 49

Chapter 4: Work, Save, Travel, Repeat — 73

Chapter 5: It´s Not the Journey, It´s the Destination — 87

Chapter 6: All About the Money — 101

Chapter 7: Get Back Home Safe   113

Chapter 8: Communication is Key   129

Chapter 9: Never Get Bored   145

Chapter 10: Don´t Let The Memories Fade Away   155

Chapter 11: More Travel, More Life   167

Chapter 12: It´s Okay to Go Alone   175

Chapter 13: My Best Experiences   195

Chapter 14: In a Nutshell   225

Introduction

I want to challenge the preconceived notions hindering people from traveling. Whether it's fear—there's too much of that these days, a lack of knowledge, availability of people to accompany you, finances, etc. There's a remedy–a solution–to all situations and obstacles, but the first step is to acknowledge the problem at hand so that you can work towards a resolution. It's imperative that we live our best life while we can. For we are never truly guaranteed how long our lives may be.

Many of us across the globe face challenges in different ways. For example, I was born and raised in South Central Los Angeles. Where I grew up, the thought of flying and seeing a foreign country was a rarity. Everyone had various obstacles and hindrances that were most times unavoidable. Traveling abroad was not an affluence that my family or friends were fortunate to have. And like so many, I felt travel would always be out of my grasp.

But… I was wrong. If you dreamed big enough, worked tirelessly, and believed in yourself, you could travel to places

Sahara Desert, Morocco

beyond your wildest dreams! And even of greater consequence, the more I traveled, the more I learned. I concluded that it was, in fact, a luxury that if planned properly, indeed, could be achieved. And, most importantly, it would not cost a fortune to experience.

I am a witness that there is so much more to life than our immediate environment. This book is written to provide insight, understanding, and enlightenment of the world at large. I dedicate this book to all those who want to travel but just don't know where to start. This book is for you!

CHAPTER 1:

The World to Explore

And then there is the most dangerous risk of all — the risk of spending your life not doing what you want on the bet you can buy yourself the freedom to do it later.
— *Randy Komisar*

Cool night winds blew through the canopy creaking and twisting the trees and grasses as I awoke. It was 3:30a.m., and I felt the breeze caress tiny hairs on the back of my neck. I stood groggily listening to the African birds' caw and the insect's chirp. As I washed my face preparing to go on the adventure flight of a lifetime, it finally hit me—I had spent the night in an arboreal safari in….Africa!

It was dark as pitch all about me as I looked into the wondrous forest, escorted by my personal butler. Immersed in wonder, I peered amongst the bending branches of several ageless trees near the river where I camped. I may have heard the scream of a baboon and the bellow of a hippo sound out near me. For certain, I heard the rushing and splashing of the river while waiting for my guide to come get me as I sat in the waiting area. They were taking me for a flight by balloon across Maasai Mara. Never in my life did I think I would ride a hot air balloon in the motherland! I looked out to a night sky illuminated by starlight in this vast region, I shook with nervous energy from the enormity of this powerful, noxious, euphoric, and dream-like moment.

"Are you ready, Miss?" My tour guide announced as he arrived. I turned from looking to the celestial trees and nodded YES. Then, off we went into the beauty of the morning night.

We drove in the vehicle winding around potholes and avoiding animals scurrying in our path. The drive took no longer than thirty minutes. We made it to the balloon drop destination and still I was stunned by what I was about to do. I, Morgan Linson, was about to ride a hot air balloon into the clouds above Kenya. I'd see the pristine beauty of an ancient landscape of green mountains, wild blue rivers, and all manner of animals. Up to this point, as I was given safety instructions, all of this had been a wondrous dream. But now, I've made this dream of dreams possible. I was 10,000 miles away from home, about to go into the morning sky accompanied by no one I knew. Yet, so grateful to be exactly where I was at that very moment.

I walked toward the balloon's basket and looked up to the towering structure with its blue fire blazing, filling our balloon with hot air for lift. As I was ushered inside the basket, I felt the firmness of the structure. I felt the coldness of the steel and the coarse texture of the basket's housing. I heard the creak of the interior. I heard the nervous and excited whispers of everyone onboard.

Looking out into the burgeoning sky on the verge of an epic morning, I wondered;

How many people have made this same journey? Were these previous travelers brave enough to experience this alone as I am and thinking as I did? Were they just as overwhelmed? Could they have experienced all the unbridled anticipation, fear, and exhilaration as they too had stood in this same spot? A spot—as my knees shake and my body trembles, that I'm standing now, preparing to ascend to the morning sky!

Intensely and curiously, I studied the straps that tethered the balloon to prevent its release. As I was directed to follow safety instructions, I continued to observe the process and preparation to fly in a balloon. I almost jumped out of my skin as our balloon driver cranked up the roaring heat to prepare for our ascent. The basket was secured and the men in charge of releasing the balloon prepared to do just that. I heard the creaking of straps and the

Maasai Mara National Park, Kenya

twisting of ropes as the balloon filled with heated air. I saw the bluish-orange flames ignited again by our driver to further inflate our balloon. I braced and secured myself shuddering in disbelief and exhilarated by what I was about to do—ascend across the heavens to the stars by myself amongst all of these strangers!

We lifted, and even in the waning light I watched as the earth below me became tiny as we made our lift. Trees became dots in my eyes and the animals below us looked like ants. As we continued our climb in the first rays of morning light, I witnessed the sun rise in all its glory with the bluest of skies. The sky itself was crystal clear and I saw land for miles. Overwhelmed, grasping for some semblance of reality, I embraced what was happening to me! It truly was in real time and so surreal. I had the greatest view of the motherland—cradle to civilization. It was breathtaking having a bird's eye view over acres of immense vistas.

It truly was an Ultimate Experience!

Life is not only to be lived, it is to be experienced.

One thing is for sure–DEATH, and two things are for certain… LIFE is short, and TIME waits for no one. If you desire to experience the world by way of travel, I encourage you to do so at your earliest convenience. Plan, save, and execute. So many people spend their whole lives solely working and/or taking care of a family, then look up one day and time has escaped them.

When we pass on, eventually we all must, shall our very existence drift forgotten across the immeasurable and immemorial expanse of time? How many of us have been asleep at the wheel in life? How many of us have spent our whole life on a hamster wheel, day in and day out? Only to look up one day and realize time has moved past us. Believe it or not, no matter what age you are currently, it's never too late to experience the world.

Take hold and live the best memories of the world. Live the best life that you can! Fill your heart with the joys of travel and the mysteries of desire. Even if you are not able to physically get on a plane while traveling, take a scenic road trip if you will. Travel is defined as going from one place to another. Abort the misconception that travel is only valid if it is in a foreign place. The art of travel is exposure to new views of not only people, places and things, but life in general. I encourage you to experience it for yourself, at your earliest convenience before you are impaired or hobbled by inevitable age.

Therefore, I begin our first lesson of three important steps to follow in order to obtain the Ultimate Experience;

1. **Plan.** Plan ahead months or even years in advance, if necessary.
2. **Save.** Save, Save, Save and then save some more.
3. **Execute.** Put the planning and money together. It's time to get things moving.

Remember:
Every day you put off travel you miss out on an experience.

I have never been into materialistic and tangible things, but more so big on seeking the purchase of excursions that provide me an experience and a feeling of pleasure. I believe in the old adage: You can't take it with you when you are gone. I absolutely enjoy being in the moment whether it's the feel of a cool beach wind or the blanketing heat of an exotic desert. Traveling gives me such a euphoria. These are the instances where acquiring a feeling of pleasure is most profound.

There is a famous quote that runs through my head constantly. One I'm sure your familiar with;

Travel is the only thing you buy that makes you richer.

Personally, it is the exhilaration behind travel that keeps me motivated to keep exploring the world. It has just been simply and plainly the curiosity of learning how people live in different countries that has kept me driven to plan my travels. Galvanized by this approach, I have managed to travel solo across the globe in times when no one else was available to travel with me. Though I was alone, I had the sweetest time of my life. Traveling has most certainly left a mark on the kind of person I am, and the kind of life I aspire to live, which is a life of freedom.

Most of my friends and family are locked into their daily lives. Most have settled down, had children and don't travel often. Waiting around for an annual trip to the safest, cheapest and most convenient destination is not for me. It is unreasonable in my mind to not experience the kind of adventurous travel that I am attracted to. Therefore, instead of waiting for a friend to find the time in their schedule, or a partner willing to travel with me, I have taken over the reins of my life and travel solo often.

Solo travel, without a doubt, can be nerve-racking. It most certainly has its pros and cons, but the pros always outweigh the cons in my judgment. Some of my favorite pros are planning, flexibility, selecting desired destinations and tours, and setting my own budget, among other things. Cons that arise are higher expenses because you don't have anyone to split the cost with, safety precautions, loneliness, etc. Adding to the unease, is planning and coordinating your itinerary when you have no prior travel experience doing so.

Traveling alone was a decision I made solely because I never wanted to be selfish. It's not in my nature to pressure anyone to travel with me when they have other responsibilities and obligations. It's only right to take into consideration that not everyone has the money, freedom, time, or even the same interest to travel. However, there is a small community of people who do. My suggestion is to figure out what kind of travel style suits you best (i.e., partner, group travel, solo, etc). Many travelers join travel groups with like-minded people that don't like traveling solo, and they thoroughly enjoy it. My best advice is to figure out what you like, and do you!

I cannot mislead you about the pearls and perils of travel. I most certainly will not lie to you and tell you that everything involving travel is rainbows and bliss. Such is the nature of life sometimes—expect the unexpected. I have had unexpected things arise while traveling. However, each of those encounters with problems involved a situation where I lacked fundamental knowledge.

I wrote this book to inspire, encourage, and empower people to travel. I want you to have the best adventure ever while on your journey. Moreover, I don't want you to encounter problems that may sideline your adventure. I'm here to reach out my hand to help you avoid obstacles that could limit your enjoyment. Which is why I want to give you a strategy plan ahead of time so that you are properly prepared.

Conclusion

To recap my travel philosophy, one thing is for sure–DEATH, and two things are for certain… LIFE is short, and TIME waits for no one. If you desire to experience all the world has to offer by way of travel, I encourage you to do so at your earliest convenience.

Now let's move forward and explore further our wonderful, and exciting world. How many countries are there for that matter? What are all the names of these countries? Let's explore all these questions together, shall we? Read on, fellow traveler.

CHAPTER 2:

Starting from the Basics

I haven't been everywhere, but it's on my list.
— ***Susan Sontag***

Now, if you are a first-time traveler or even just thinking about traveling, then there are certain facts that you need to know before getting started. The most important, is that the world is a vast place full of things to explore.

Figure 1: World Map-Illustration of Earth's seven continents and its countries.

We live in a big world, with countries spread at each corner of the globe. There are 7 continents in the world, Asia, Africa, Europe, North America, South America, Australia and Antarctica. Based on the size of each continent, Asia is the largest, with the rest as follows:

No.	Continent	Area in Km²
1.	Asia	44,579,000
2.	Africa	30,370,000
3.	North America	24,709,000
4.	South America	17,840,000
5.	Antarctica	14,000,000
6.	Europe	10,180,000
7.	Australia	8,600,000

Figure 2: Listing of Seven Continents and Size Kilometers Squared (KM²)

Another way of distributing the continents is by their population. The list of continents from most populated to least populated is as follows:

No.	Continent	Population (YTD Jan 2022)
1.	Asia	4,689,397,900
2.	Africa	1,387,393,400
3.	Europe	746,129,000
4.	North America	597,677,700
5.	South America	435,083,400
6.	Australia	43,398,700
7.	Antarctica	No permanent residents

Figure 3: Seven continents with population density as of year-to-date (YTD) January 2022.

The world is 71% water with the oceans making up the majority of that percentage. Major oceans are defined as those that flow between land bodies. These oceans are the Atlantic, Pacific, Indian, Arctic and Southern Arctic Oceans. On a smaller scale, the oceans are further divided into seas. The top 10 of the largest seas that are a point of attraction for tourists are:

No.	Sea	Area (KM^2)
1.	Mediterranean Sea	2,965,800
2.	Caribbean Sea	2,718,200

3.	South China Sea	2,319,000
4.	Bering Sea	2,291,900
5.	Gulf of Mexico	1,592,800
6.	Okhotsk Sea	1,589,700
7.	East China Sea	1,249,200
8.	Hudson Bay	1,232,300
9.	the Sea of Japan (East Sea)	1,007,800
10.	Andaman Sea	797,700

Figure 4: Ten seas that are popular tourist attractions. Area size in kilometers squared (KM^2)

Even though popular tourism is mostly done in ancient cities and cultural hotspots, the seas and the oceans also have plenty to offer. They cover a much larger area than land, while providing optimal opportunities. These include extreme adventure sports such as snorkeling or free diving, scuba diving, and cliff diving. To be honest, I would rather stay on land than water, so you will rarely catch me partaking in those activities. Other, less extreme adventures are swimming, water skiing, surfing, and fishing.

The deep seas are the last frontier of exploration. We know more of the moon and the stars than the fathoms of our ocean abysses. Deep sea exploration and tourism is an additional adventure for those with the means and training to do so. What an opportunity to explore undiscovered places or ocean depths few have ventured. Keep in mind as you trek miles below the ocean's surface, that ninety four percent of living species reside in the mysterious abyss. How extraordinary it would be to view environments and creatures never before seen, but avoid getting on a submarine to do so!!!

If it is not the oceans that pique your interest, you can choose to travel to different countries as well. There are a total of 195 countries in the world.... YES, I said 195! If you are an aspiring traveler, this list of countries can help you keep a tally of those you visit as it comes to pass. An alphabetical list to make this process easier is given:

No.	Country	Visited	No.	Country	Visited
1.	Afghanistan		2.	Albania	
3.	Algeria		4.	Andorra	
5.	Angola		6.	Antigua and Barbuda	
7.	Argentina		8.	Armenia	
9.	Australia		10.	Austria	
11.	Azerbaijan		12.	Bahamas	
13.	Bahrain		14.	Bangladesh	
15.	Barbados		16.	Belarus	
17.	Belgium		18.	Belize	
19.	Benin		20.	Bhutan	
21.	Bolivia		22.	Bosnia and Herzegovina	

No.	Country	Visited	No.	Country	Visited
23.	Botswana		24.	Brazil	
25.	Brunei		26.	Bulgaria	
27.	Burkina Faso		28.	Burundi	
29.	Côte d'Ivoire		30.	Cabo Verde	
31.	Cambodia		32.	Cameroon	
33.	Canada		34.	Central African Republic	
35.	Chad		36.	Chile	
37.	China		38.	Colombia	
39.	Comoros		40.	Congo	
41.	Costa Rica		42.	Croatia	
43.	Cuba		44.	Cyprus	
45.	Czechia (Czech Republic)		46.	Democratic Republic of the Congo	
47.	Denmark		48.	Djibouti	
49.	Dominica		50.	Dominica Republic	
51.	The Democratic Republic of Timor-Leste		52.	Ecuador	
53.	Egypt		54.	El Salvador	
55.	Equatorial Guinea		56.	Eritrea	

No.	Country	Visited	No.	Country	Visited
57.	Estonia		58.	Eswatini (formerly known as Swaziland)	
59.	Ethiopia		60.	Fiji	
61.	Finland		62.	France	
63.	Gabon		64.	Gambia	
65.	Georgia		66.	Germany	
67.	Ghana		68.	Greece	
69.	Grenada		70.	Guatemala	
71.	Guinea		72.	Guinea-Bissau	
73.	Guyana		74.	Haiti	
75.	Holy See		76.	Honduras	
77.	Hungary		78.	Iceland	
79.	India		80.	Indonesia	
81.	Iran		82.	Iraq	
83.	Ireland		84.	Israel	
85.	Italy		86.	Jamaica	
87.	Japan		88.	Jordan	
89.	Kazakhstan		90.	Kenya	
91.	Kiribati		92.	Kuwait	
93.	Kyrgyzstan		94.	Laos	
95.	Latvia		96.	Lebanon	

STARTING FROM THE BASICS | 25

No.	Country	Visited	No.	Country	Visited
97.	Lesotho		98.	Liberia	
99.	Libya		100.	Liechtenstein	
101.	Lithuania		102.	Luxembourg	
103.	Madagascar		104.	Malawi	
105.	Malaysia		106.	Maldives	
107.	Mali		108.	Malta	
109.	Marshall Islands		110.	Mauritania	
111.	Mauritius		112.	Mexico	
113.	Micronesia		114.	Moldova	
115.	Monaco		116.	Mongolia	
117.	Montenegro		118.	Morocco	
119.	Mozambique		120.	Myanmar (formerly known as Burma)	
121.	Namibia		122.	Nauru	
123.	Nepal		124.	Netherlands	
125.	New Zealand		126.	Nicaragua	
127.	Niger		128.	North Korea	
129.	North Macedonia		130.	Norway	
131.	Oman		132.	Pakistan	

No.	Country	Visited	No.	Country	Visited
133.	Palau		134.	Palestine	
135.	Panama		136.	Papua New Guinea	
137.	Paraguay		138.	Peru	
139.	Philippines		140.	Poland	
141.	Portugal		142.	Qatar	
143.	Romania		144.	Russia	
145.	Rwanda		146.	Saint Kitts and Nevis	
147.	Saint Lucia		149.	Saint Vincent and the Grenadines	
149.	Samoa		150.	San Marino	
151.	São Tomé and Príncipe		152.	Saudi Arabia	
153.	Senegal		154.	Serbia	
155.	Seychelles		155.	Sierra Leone	
157.	Singapore		158.	Slovakia	
159.	Slovenia		160.	Solomon Islands	
161.	Somalia		162.	South Africa	
163.	South Korea		164.	South Sudan	
165.	Spain		166.	Sri Lanka	
167.	Sudan		168.	Suriname	

No.	Country	Visited	No.	Country	Visited
169.	Sweden		170.	Switzerland	
171.	Syria		172.	Tajikistan	
173.	Tanzania		174.	Thailand	
175.	Timor-Leste		176.	Togo	
177.	Tonga		178.	Trinidad and Tobago	
179.	Tunisia		180.	Turkey	
181.	Turkmenistan		182.	Tuvalu	
183.	Uganda		184.	Ukraine	
185.	United Arab Emirates		186.	United Kingdom	
187.	United States of America		188.	Uruguay	
189.	Uzbekistan		190.	Vanuatu	
191.	Venezuela		192.	Vietnam	
193.	Yemen		194.	Zambia	
195.	Zimbabwe				

Figure 5: A checklist of 195 countries of the world in alphabetical order.

Some Facts to Consider

When making travel plans, it is important to consider a few things beforehand. Safety and awareness should be your number one priority! Check the airline safety records, the daily safety reports of the region for travel, any medical quarantine or pandemic information, and most importantly logistics.

As a traveler, it is important to know basic facts that can help you navigate across new countries, cultures, and people that may be completely alien to you.

> **PRO TIP:**
>
> You never want to look as though you are lost and don't know your surroundings. Natives have a sense of identifying people that can be lured or exploited, so always move with purpose and intention. Every day as a solo traveler, my schedule runs off a strict itinerary (rides, guides, activities, excursions). Rather you are traveling with a companion or group, it's always better to have your days planned in order to maximize your experience and ensure you do what you came to do.

Travel Safety Check (International & Domestic Travel)

- Plan your travel routes in advance but keep it on a need to know. When too many people know where you are going, things can get tricky. Be sure to inform and share your complete itinerary with your loved ones (parents, siblings, close friend, partner).
- Avoid driving yourself if possible. Be mindful that many foreign countries drive on the opposite side of the road than your home country, so even the most seasoned driver could have a wreck. I've seen expats that had costly

STARTING FROM THE BASICS | 29

outcomes when a local driver crashed into them to garner money. Also, local drivers know—laws, shortcuts, and safety concerns, which we don't as tourists.

- Avoid driving in inclement weather conditions, nighttime, on busy weekends. Remember fog, rain, drunks, and other tourists can put you at a high risk of injury or worse.
- Be familiar with and know local road warning signs and closures.
- Always check your weather and safety reports daily. Things change in travel environments. Stay up to date. I investigate the weather during planning, so I can pack clothes appropriate to the destination climate.

Although there are 195 countries in the world, the distribution of those countries across continents remains uneven. A list of countries per continent, from highest to lowest, is given as follows:

Continent	Number of Countries
Africa	54
Asia	48
Europe	44
North America	23
Australia	14
South America	12
Antarctica	12 (countries that have claimed territory over Antarctic land)

Africa

Beginning with Africa, there are fifty-four countries and a total of approximately 1.3 billion people currently living on the continent. The largest country in Africa remains Algeria, while the highest tourism rate remains Morocco, which offers luxury as well as budget traveling options. Before traveling to Africa, you should know that there are over 3000 indigenous groups living on the continent across various territories. National borders do not necessarily mean that the ethnicity of the people is also different. For instance, the famous Maasai tribe of Africa lives in both Kenya and Tanzania, which is personally one of my favorite tribes to date.

Morgan the Explorer (my travel inspired YouTube channel) highlights the wonders of Africa with the mission to erase the misconception and false narratives that the motherland only embodies poverty, disease and despair. Africa is by far my favorite continent to visit on earth. Believe it or not, Africa is the richest continent in the world when it comes to natural resources. Countries all over the face of the planet have robbed and exploited those very resources and benefited tremendously from Africa's fortune.

Like most people, I, too, allowed propaganda to delay my visit. Now, having visited 17 countries on the African continent, I'm here to tell you… it is an experience of a lifetime! I am an avid animal lover, so an enchanting African safari always gives me

Dakar, Senegal

a gleeful feeling of ecstasy. Not to mention, the mind blowing preservation of traditional culture that has been upheld and modernly practiced is admirable. Every shade of melanin and every texture of hair exists in Africa. Beauty is not only skin deep, it flows through joyful spirits which are always welcoming. The undeniable feeling of gratitude is what I feel every time I step foot off the plane onto the ground of the motherland. Kenya was the first country that I visited in Africa, and it is by far my favorite country in the world.

Asia

Being the largest continent on our planet, Asia has a lot to offer. Upwards of 4.7 billion people live in Asia, and the continent shares an indistinct border with Europe. This means that countries like Russia, Turkey, Georgia, and Kazakhstan, are also included as part of Asia. But, surprisingly, traveling there will give you a mixture of the cultures from region to region. Apart from this, language, religion and belief systems in Asia also offer an additional layer of travel experience. There are the ancient Buddhist temples across the Himalayas. Journeying further across Asia's mountains, forests, and vistas, you'll find Hindu temples in India, or Mughal mosques in Pakistan. All these can offer the mystery of ancient chants, the wonder of their architecture and many more new biographies in your travels.

Taj Mahal, Agra, India

In contrast, the social and political history of the Imperial House of Japan, the Ottoman Empire in Turkey, Mughals in India, Mesopotamian Empire in Jordan, etc., all offer a different outlook on the larger and richer history that the region has to offer. Especially in Turkey, the oldest ruins to date have recently been discovered to the excitement of the world. I've had the personal pleasure of traveling in Asia and it was nothing short of amazing. My most recent trip to Asia was to Japan, and I can honestly say that I was pleasantly surprised at how much I loved my vacation.

Europe

The European continent has 44 countries, which can be distinctly divided into the West and East when it comes to the economy, politics, culture and even climate. There are 28 countries, mostly in the Western part of Europe, that belong to the European Union. As a traveler, visas can be obtained for the Schengen Area inside the EU. Although, it depends on your passport. Traveling to Europe, you can either decide to travel within budget, which includes countries such as Hungary, Slovenia or Portugal. Then there's the exclusive luxury tourist spots to visit, like Monte Carlo, the French Riviera, and Greek Islands.

Other stunning and exotic European travel destinations to check out include the pristine coastal areas of Ibiza. While the regions of Sardinia, Ölüdeniz Beach, and Vik Beach are among the most popular. However, this does not mean that land-locked areas in Europe do not offer tourism-related activities. There are the exquisite ancient and vintage countries of Belarus, Switzerland, Vatican City, Slovakia, Moldova, and Liechtenstein. These grandeur places offer fine cuisine, treks across winding mountains, fine wines, and rich, historical museums.

North America

North America has twenty-three countries in total from the towering Canadian Rockies, on into the mountains, jungles, and coasts of the Yucatan. The obvious and accessible travel spots for most travelers is the United States. Within the U.S. fifty states, you'll find endless adventure and opportunities to make lasting memories. Deciding which state to visit may be the toughest of all your decisions. Again, it will depend on your preference about how and why you want to travel the U.S. Or if you are like me, and live here, exploring your own backyard isn't a bad idea at all.

You can opt to head to the Pacific coast for sun and fun in California. While there, check out Los Angeles for the palm trees and beaches. Or head down Rodeo Drive where you might catch a glimpse of the Hollywood sign along the way. But, if the city isn't your thing, and the outdoors calls you to the wild, then the breathtaking Pacific Northwest may do the trick. With its ancient redwoods and roaring rivers, it'll be easy to lose yourself in the peace and quiet of nature.

If the Sunshine state isn't your thing, head over to the East Coast and historic District of Columbia. Situated on the east bank of the Potomac River, and bordering Maryland and Virginia, Washington D.C. is the United States capital. While there, enjoy the pageantry of the cherry blossoms, on your walk from The Reflecting Pool toward many memorial sites. You will find many museums and sites to educate you on the history of the U.S. The Smithsonian Museum is particularly one of my favorites.

The United States has many national parks, with millions of acres of pristine wilderness, and roaring crystal-clear rivers for you to explore. Journeying south you can check the windswept plains of Texas and eat real, sizzling barbecue. Or head east from Texas into the heart of the mysterious, shadowed swamps of the Atchafalaya Basin. There you can almost taste the cayenne spiced delicacy of Cajun country—crawfish! Or stare in wonder into New Orleans at the grandeur of the mighty Mississippi River. Jazz music, bars that never close, and Creole gumbo await.

But if politics, media, and ecology are not your thing, roll the dice, and take a chance that luck is on your side in the state of Nevada. You'll find cities

Tulum, Mexico

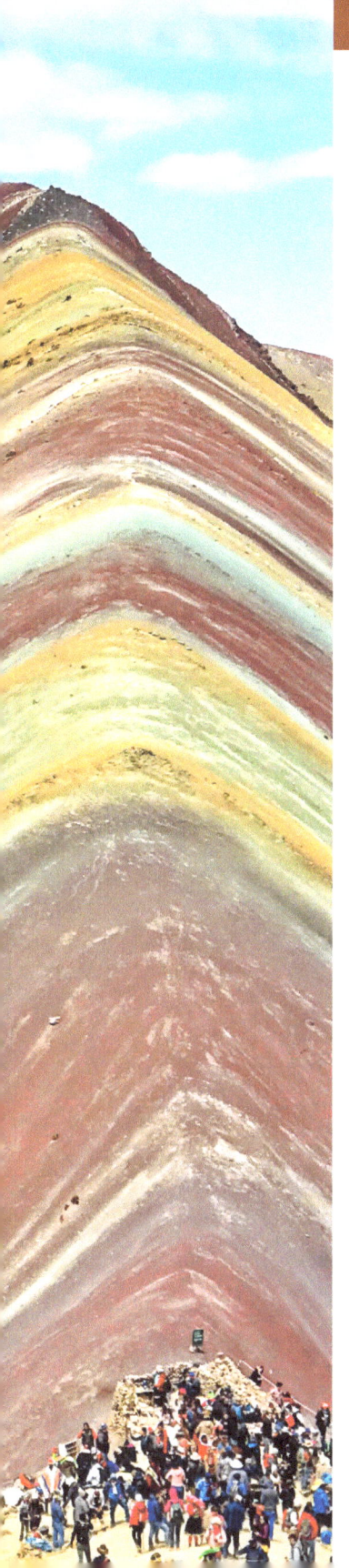

like Reno and Las Vegas solely built for one thing—gambling. Famous casinos, five-star dining, and all manner of debauchery await. And remember the Las Vegas motto;

What happens in Vegas… stays in Vegas.

If you survive Las Vegas, head East Coast to the Garden State–New York. You could check out a fashion show, a concert in City Park, or an art gallery exhibit. If sports are your thing, the state has seasonal baseball, marathons, and football games to entertain. The city of New York boasts some of the best Broadway plays, memorable musicals, and many of the most infamous hotels for you to visit.

If you do not want to visit the US, then other countries like Canada, Mexico, Costa Rica and Cuba also provide several cultural hubs, with geographical areas, including mountains, highlands, rivers and coastal areas. Countries in the Caribbean are the place to be to catch the sun, party, witness amazing blue beaches, eat, drink and be merry. Islands like Jamaica, Turks, and Bahamas, just to name a few all pass the vibe check and are must-visit destinations.

South America

Although South America only has 14 countries, with 12 countries and 2 dependencies, it can still be an attractive destination for coastal, ecological and cultural travelers. You can visit the Incan Empire's historical sites in South America, while Machu Picchu, Iguazu Falls and the Amazon Forest are all wonders of the natural world. So much history has been preserved and upheld, which is vitally impactful and respectable for the ancestors who paved the way. The food in every country that I have visited was remarkably tasteful and delicious. The diversity of various adventures is endless. I must tell you that when I travel within South America, I get the best bang for my buck. Literally everything is so reasonably priced and worth every dollar. Not to mention, the natives are so welcoming and nice to tourists, they will make you feel right at home regardless of your nationality. My first solo trip ever was to Peru, and it was magical.

Australia

The continent of Australia is a point of attraction for travelers who seek warmer climates and blue oceans. The Gold Coast, Byron Bay and Mamanuca Islands of Fiji are extremely beautiful, with pleasing climates, and high-end island resorts to offer a good time for anyone who visits. Mountains in New Zealand also have much to offer, with Roy's Peak, Mount Ngauruhoe, Mount Taranaki, etc., providing visitors with awe-inspiring experiences. The nightlife of major Australian, and New Zealand cities is another source of attraction, with various bars, eateries and pubs for travelers to choose from. Another fact to consider when traveling to Australia, is The Ghan, which is a famous train ride that takes visitors from the North to South, with major cities like Sydney and Melbourne in the South and smaller cities of Darwin and Katherine in the north. I have yet to visit the continent, but it's definitely on my to-do list.

Antarctica

Antarctica is the southernmost, coldest, and windiest place on Earth. Traveling to the most isolated place on the planet requires more planning than simply visiting a city in Europe. Solo trips largely remain uncommon for Antarctica. But even in a group, you can plan voyages in late spring and early fall, as the sea ice usually opens up to allow access to the mainland. The scenery in Antarctica will be unlike any of the other continents because of its harsh, cold climate. Unique flora and fauna specific to the region can only be found in this place. It has been one of my most desirable destinations to travel to and currently a bucket list adventure of mine. However, it will most likely have to be done by cruise because Antarctica does not have any developed public-access airports, nor does it have hotels. There are many cruise companies that offer year-round excursions, but it can get very expensive.

Conclusion

The world is truly a vast and mysterious place with its 7 continents and 195 different countries with limitless languages, customs and cultures in each country. Researching ahead of time the country you are traveling to will save you many headaches and minimize challenges in the long run. Do your homework and as always plan ahead. And as a constant reminder:

1. **Plan.** Plan ahead maybe months or years in advance. Under this know the risks, the safety precautions, and the plan for the country you are visiting!
2. **Save.** Again, save every penny maybe months or years in advance.
3. **Execute.** You put the planning and money together. It's time to get things moving.

Traveling abroad has its share of risks, but being prepared and knowledgeable can make all the difference in the world. As I mentioned in the safety data, driving yourself in certain countries is one of just a few precautions. The injury that you avoid, or the life you save not being foolhardy and reckless... may be your own.

Are you excited about journeying out to that mysterious island in the middle of nowhere? What is the process for getting a visa? Read on fellow travelers as we explore further all these questions.

CHAPTER 3:

Get Ready

Travel leaves you speechless, then turns you into a storyteller.
– ***Ibn-e-Battuta***

As exciting as traveling may be, it can turn into an adventure or a disaster depending upon your preparation. When it comes to traveling, planning for a trip in advance is essential. Whether it be researching the touring spots of your travel destination or making a list of items to pack, planning your days ahead of time is a necessity.

Following the *ULTIMATE EXPERIENCE* guidelines, we should plan accordingly. Expect the unexpected! Now that you've researched the popular attractions of the city you will be traveling to, learning and exploring all the safety data of the country you'll be visiting is just as vital. Guides, logistics, cool places to see, and any changes— sandstorms in the Sahara Desert, hurricanes in the Caribbean, etc., that you might want to avoid.

There are many reasons why it is important to program your trip properly in order to make it the best and safest. The goal is to avoid finding yourself in any challenging situations. The solution to potential undesirable circumstances you might come up against while traveling is to know about it ahead of time and avoid it if at all possible. Trust me, I understand the devastation of a highly anticipated travel approaching and you end up not going because of some natural disaster or security issue…. but don't trip! It's better to be safe than sorry. Always check on the foreign country you are going to visit before you arrive.

> **TIP:**
>
> Furthering research on any place is good practice. Having a few go to sites for information is even better, especially if you have an issue. Foreign Embassies of Washington D.C., the Foreign Consular Offices in the United States. Here are some links below that are useful in case you are caught in an emergency overseas.

State Link: https://travel.state.gov/content/travel/en/international-travel/emergencies.html

Government Link: https://www.usembassy.gov/

There is a famous saying, **Always expect the unexpected.** It simply means that we should always be prepared for anything, because trouble doesn't inform us before it comes knocking on our door. When traveling, anything can happen. You could miss your flight due to a catastrophic emergency like a natural disaster, or simply because you overslept. In the case of an emergency, a great safety tool to take advantage of is to enroll in the US Department of State's free S.T.E.P program before you go on any international trip. STEP stands for Smart Traveler Enrollment Program, which is a free service that allows US citizens and nationals traveling and living abroad to enroll in their trip to the nearest US Embassy or Consulate in the country that they are traveling to. Enrolling in the program makes it easier for the State Department to find you in the case of an emergency, such as a natural disaster or terrorist attack. Being in the STEP program puts you in the database, which makes you more accessible to locate and provide help or even evacuation in the case of a serious situation.

S.T.E.P. Link: https://step.state.gov/step/

In order to avoid situations like missing your flight due to poor time management, a key remedy I can provide you with is to be punctual and reach the airport early. Practicing this might waste some of your precious time, but it will help you stay stress-free.

You could be at the airport, waiting in line for your boarding pass, and realize that you forgot your passport (you may have left it locked in the safe of the room you just checked out of). Whatever the cause may be, it is vital to make sure you have everything you need before you arrive. One of the ways you can avoid that is by keeping a checklist of everything that needs to be prepared before you embark on your journey and when

you are on your way back home. The list may include essential things you need to travel, such as your passport and proof of vaccination or a negative PCR test result (if applicable), items you need to pack, and checking post-covid travel requirements for your destination. Luckily, the covid pandemic is over and the regulations to enter and exit countries are less restrictive. I traveled a lot during the pandemic, and it was extremely hectic. Although things are nearly back to normal, still be sure to check each country you plan to visit for health screening requirements.

Pre-Travel Checklist:

- Passport
- Credit card, debit card, and designated amount of cash
- Charger cords with plugs
- Universal Converter adapters. It is really important to have adapters while traveling because many countries use different power outlets.
- Buy travel insurance (especially if your schedule is always fluctuating or have an unsteady lifestyle)
- Portable power banks that have long battery life
- Medication (must haves are anti-diarrhea, pain relievers, antihistamines, cough/cold medications. I even have my doctor prescribe me antibiotics in case I get food poisoning)
- Required immunization for specific countries (consult a travel health specialist)
- Sunblock and bug spray

- Appropriate shoes (for women a neutral heel, sandals, tennis shoes)
- Appropriate clothes based on the weather.

Now you are on your way. What things should you remember while traveling and at your hotel? Well, here's another checklist below to help.

In-Travel Checklist:

- Have an agent, host or guide coordinate transportation, hotels, and the driver or guide-if needed. I usually arrange certified transportation from my hotel to pick me up or take Uber if it's available in that country (you can research before arrival if Uber is available.)
- Make it a habit to know and sit near emergency exits on planes and vehicles. Don't wait until an emergency to learn where they are.
- Know your fire escape routes even in the dark. Again, don't wait until an actual fire.
- Be careful giving personal information to locals (travel arrangements, room numbers, occupation, etc.)
- Be aware that expats are favored targets of criminals, so travel with intention and purpose.
- Avoid arguments with the local populace. It could cause issues.
- Keep backup copies of all important documents—passports, visas, etc. NEVER take your passport with you on excursions or out roaming as a tourist, because if you

lose it, or it gets stolen… you are in trouble. I always leave my passport in the safe at my hotel and take only a copy (make a copy before you travel). Please note that some tours require you to have the original copy of your passport to participate in certain tours or enter some archeological sites, so ask your guide or tour company before your daily tour departure. Make sure to get your passport out of the safe at your hotel before you leave to go to the airport.

- Keep credit and bank cards separated and a back-up amount of cash hidden in the event you lose your wallet.
- Don't exchange your money at the airport, due to higher than average rates unless necessary.
- Do not carry unmarked prescription bottles. Police sometimes are looking for an easy pay day, in some countries. In all seriousness, you don't want to give anyone a reason to incriminate you. Please be mindful that Marijuana is legal in some States in the US, but is illegal in many countries around the world… so please do not take it with you while traveling.
- Hotel phones, mail, and the internet are monitored at hotels, hostiles, etc. Always assume someone is listening. When using public Wi-Fi, be mindful of browsing personal bank accounts and exposing sensitive information. In today's day and age, the internet is not safe.
- When you can, monitor the drinks being poured and the food you are served. Always be cautious. I like to eat at restaurants that are established and have a lot of

customers. It's always a good idea to eat locally and indulge in traditional food, but be mindful about sanitation. I tend to stay away from street food (although it is usually the best tasting), because I fear getting sick while on vacation. Food poisoning is a real thing and if it happens to you it can result in hospitalization depending on the organism ingested. Always bring with you anti-diarrhea medication and if you have a primary doctor, ask for travel antibiotics in case you have a severe case of food poisoning.

- Hanging the "Make Up Room" sign on your room door is probably a bad idea at some hotels. Use the "Do Not Disturb" sign. Contact housekeeping in advance verbally if you are going out, when you want your room cleaned.

- Sometimes if the country that I'm visiting has a good public transportation system and is fairly safe, I engage in public transportation. Not only is it extremely cheap, but it gives you an opportunity to experience the culture of the city.

PRO TIP:

Always carry an outfit with you in your carry-on luggage. Especially, be sure to carry anything that is important with you in your carry-on or personal bag. Never put your iPad or laptop in your checked bag. Also, label your luggage so it can be easier to identify. If your luggage is lost, having luggage easy to identify would always be very helpful to the airline.

Indian Ocean, Maldives

True Story:

I was leaving India on my way to Sri Lanka for an extended layover before heading to the Maldives. We arrived in Colombo, Sri Lanka, and guess what…. the airline mistakenly left my luggage in India. I was devastated because all of my good clothes were in my checked luggage. Luckily, I had my carry-on luggage with me which had my toiletries, makeup, a few lounge pieces of clothing and some underwear, so I could at least be comfortable. However, I was on my way to Maldives in freaking 36 hours. I needed all my bomb bathing suits for our amazing overwater bungalow stay. The Sri Lanka airline claimed they would get me my luggage from India before I departed from Sri Lanka, but that never happened! I didn't receive my luggage until the second day in Maldives. What saved me was that I at least had some items to hold me over until my luggage arrived, which is a practice I have been doing for a long time now and even more since that situation occurred. When possible, always carry a change of clothes and important items with you in your carry-on luggage or bag.

How to Plan a Trip

Since we have already discussed the importance of planning and preparing for a trip, I will now elaborate on planning for an entire trip and the best ways to do it. Furthermore, I will discuss how you can design your trip according to what suits you, your personality, traveling style, and preferences.

1. Travel Destination

Though it may sound easy, deciding on a specific travel destination can be tricky. Sure, there are probably a few places that you have always had on your bucket list, but when the time comes, deciding which one(s) to travel to can be hard to decide. First, you need to know how many days or weeks you or your group can take off work and other duties. Secondly, you need to decide whether you can travel to one country or a couple of them according to your budget. I always maximize my travels when I fly to another continent by visiting the neighboring countries, because it's way cheaper than going home and finding another time to travel all the way back. Especially when I go to Africa, due to the travel time being so long, I take a flight or cross borders by car to a desirable neighboring country. To give you an example, it may take me 18 hours to get to Kenya from Los Angeles, but it only takes one hour to get from Kenya to Tanzania…. So of course, I'll hop on a quick flight and get it into my trip. Just last summer, I flew into Ghana, then crossed the border to Togo by car, and then I crossed the border to Benin from Togo all in one trip. You just have to do your research and verify which borders are open, if you need a visa to enter and if so does it need to be purchased ahead of time or upon arrival.

I personally get a lot of travel inspiration from social media. I am a very visual person and love to see people's true experiences, which is why I got into YouTube because I also like seeing vlogs.

As mentioned earlier, most of my trips have been solo. The reason being is my understanding that not everyone can get up and move on my time. Being in my mid-30s, 90% of my friends have children, which is a beautiful thing. It would be selfish and delusional for me to think that they should abandon their children to come explore with me. Also, financially for most people traveling is not a priority or in their budget, and that too is okay. My comprehension that the world doesn't revolve around me gave me the courage and determination to get out in the world and see it for myself. When traveling solo, I can travel according to my convenience.

As much as I love my solo trips and freedom, hopefully in the near future, I too will become a mother. I do believe taking time off from traveling for maternity and the first year after birth will annoy the hell out of me, but your girl is getting up there in age so time is of the essence. If (or should I say when) I hop on the motherhood train, as soon as my child is walking, he or she will become my travel buddy! My parents never took me and my siblings on trips and vacations, so I am eager to break that cycle and share the world with my children when the time comes.

2. Traveling Style

I have traveled around the globe in almost every way. There are many ways people travel, and below are a few traveling styles you can check out that might suit you.

■ Independent

The most common way people travel is the independent style of travel. It is where you, along with your partner or group, follow a pre-set itinerary. In this style, your flights and accommodation are pre-booked and/or booking upon arrival. You get to enjoy yourself and your companions however you like. On a day when you feel like relaxing and resting, you can cancel your other plans and do just that.

■ Escorted Tours

The opposite of independent tours, escorted tours include a tour guide and a day-to-day planned trip. Therefore, this kind of traveling arrangement is most convenient for those traveling for the first time. Although I personally do not like traveling this way, I have seen many people feeling at ease with it the most. Travel companies generally put together trips like this for a set price and make all the plans. For people that are afraid of solo traveling and don't have anyone to travel with, this may be your best option to get your feet wet.

■ Backpacker

This style of touring is different from all the rest. With this, one can travel on a minimal budget and for longer durations, allowing you to visit many destinations in one stretch. I'm sure a lot of people, along with myself, do not prefer traveling this way, but I find this technique to be the most adventurous and full of enriching experiences. It's literally you and your backpack with only the necessary items one feels is needed, which generally only consists of a wallet, passport and a few articles of clothing.

■ Solo

This travel style is for people who do not mind being alone and travel sporadically. Unlike group tours, this traveling style gives you the flexibility of doing things according to your specific likes and taste. Traveling solo you will have the luxury of controlling your own budget and itinerary. You have the autotomy to pick and choose each and every detail, as well as make changes as you please. Solo travel has become my designated way of travel nowadays. This travel style has increased my confidence, decreased my fears, empowered me mentally, enhanced my spirituality, gave me self-actualization, helped me regulate my emotional state, assisted me in learning my true self, and so much more. Solo travel isn't for everyone, but for those that are interested in it…. I have a special chapter in the book just for you!

3. Season and Climate

One of the key points to be reviewed before finalizing your time and date of travel is the season you will travel to your desired destination. For example, if you want to ski during your journey, you must make sure there will be snow and, thus, winter. Another aspect that must be thought of is the typical climate and weather of the place you are traveling to. Is it hot? Then you must pack items that will protect you from the scorching heat. Is it rainy? Then do not forget to include your raincoat and an umbrella in your luggage. Finally, the most crucial factor of all, will it be a suitable season for you to carry out all the activities that you have planned? Summer months may be July and August in the U.S., but in Australia during that same time it's Winter. Before confirming your travel dates, all these things must be considered.

4. Prices of Air Travel

If you know when you will travel, it is crucial to check the airfare pricing before finalizing the dates. The reason is that flights vary at different times of the year, depending upon the demand for travel at that time. Having planned your whole trip and then realizing that the airfare is way out of your budget at the last moment is the worst feeling, so to avoid that, make sure to do proper research. The first thing I purchase when planning a trip is my flight. Once I have a confirmed seat on a plane, I know it's a GO!

The website that I use to book my flights is www.momondo.com. Momondo also has a downloadable app for all smart phones.

Many people use Skyscanner, Hopper, Kayak, Expedia, Google flights, Orbitz, Cheap flights, etc. To be completely honest, I look at them all for comparison… but I always end up going with Momondo, because they are usually the cheapest and I never have problems booking (but that's just me)! Ultimately, choose whichever site is the cheapest and most reliable. Just note that they are cheap because they are third-party companies. Please realize that because you are booking through a third party, you are not confirmed until you get a confirmation number from the airline. Once I get the airline confirmation, I immediately verify it with the airline using the app. I love using apps, and keep them downloaded for easy access.

If your schedule is subject to change, do yourself a favor and get travel insurance. Travel insurance will cover you if you need to cancel your flight, if your bags are lost or stolen, medical coverage in the event you become ill, etc. I will not tell you a lie and say that I always get travel insurance, because I don't. But in most cases I do. If you are a new traveler, please get some insurance.

PRO TIP:

It's always safest to book directly through the airline which you are traveling with, because of the rewards and sky miles. Most importantly, if something goes wrong you will not have to worry about dealing with a third party. Also, if you use your credit card that has perks, you will get 3x to 5x the credit miles. My favorite airline is and will always be Delta!

5. Accommodation

After having decided where you want to travel, there is nothing more essential than making arrangements for your accommodation in the host country. The first step is to search for different types of lodging options (hotels, Airbnb, hostels, private rooms).

As of lately, I have been booking directly through my AMEX travel membership. Before I was an AMEX card holder, I used www.booking.com to book most of my hotel accommodations. Doing so, I have become a Genius member, which is Booking's loyalty program. I enjoy discounts and travel rewards worldwide. Regardless of what company you book your hotels through, my advice is for you to use the same one every time you book in order to accumulate points and rewards.

To be transparent, I refrain from staying at an Airbnb when I travel alone. The reason being is, I like feeling secure in hotels that have a front desk, security guards, security cameras, people traffic, etc. Staying at an Airbnb is not regulated enough for me and sometimes poses risks like mysterious neighbors, unknown hidden cameras, and carbon monoxide hazards.

Thanks to the internet, you can find countless accommodation options in a matter of minutes. Of course, listings are usually available in every city and country. You should always check reviews by previous travelers who have stayed in these places.

Before finalizing your reservation, always compare the price offer. There are plenty of websites and apps out there that allow you to compare the prices of different hotels until you decide the one best suited for you. I keep mentioning hotels, but it can be any accommodation style you choose.

Planning before taking a trip might be challenging, but it is essential for having a good time. Despite all the initial troubles you might face when outlining your trip, it is necessary, and the benefits far outweigh the hassle. With the help of the aforementioned steps, your trip will be secure, stress-free, and enjoyable.

Conclusion

To recap, traveling is so exciting and thrilling, especially journeying to places you have never been before! Keep in mind however, as exciting as traveling may be, it can be the ultimate adventure or the worst disaster with improper safety and logistics planning. Plan, plan, and re-check the plan in advance is imperative. Whether it be researching the touring spots of your travel destination or making a list of items to pack, planning your days ahead of time always comes in handy. So, as we continue our journey let us recall. When planning, always expect the unexpected so you will be prepared for the unlikely event of something going wrong.

The website resources can assist you to know the current logistics concerns, best places to stay, best places to eat, or weather reports of the region you'll be exploring. Websites, such as the embassy, can give you an accurate picture of the safety concerns or assist you with all sorts of advisories once you are there. It's good practice to check in with them on occasion too.

Pre-travel checklists, in-travel checklists, and even a post travel checklist are valuable planning and safety tools. They are helpful reminders and good habits to prevent lost items or incidents.

As referenced previously, travel planning needs to be carefully thought out. From the place that will give you the ultimate experience at the right time of year or month to avoid unruly crowds or bad weather, to the best routes or means of travel. Other parts of the travel plans should include the safest and most desirable accommodation, as well as delicious food which may include local mom and pop restaurants in many cases.

Finally, the style of traveling you prefer to do—independent versus group travel—should be planned out and fit your desired needs. Solo and backpacking traveling is great and sometimes a rewarding experience in itself, but there are risks you should research with them. Do your research, plan accordingly, and have a great adventure.

Cairo, Egypt

Okay, you've thoroughly researched your desired destination, have a flight plan ready, your hotel picked out, your travel style determined, and double-checked the U.S. Embassies daily reports of the region for the last couple of months. So…now what to do?!

It's time to save up the money to go. You aren't going to wait forty years before heading to your *Ultimate Experience*… Are you? You will be able to go now if you follow my strategy for saving to live out your dreams. Explore further with me fellow travelers as we discuss strategies for having the means to go anywhere you want in the world.

CHAPTER 4:

Work, Save, Travel, Repeat

I work very hard, and I play very hard. I'm grateful for life. And I live it - I believe life loves the liver of it. I live it.
— *Maya Angelou*

Do you want to travel the world? You want to minimize your costs to maximize the amount of cash you'll have on your trip? Well, remember the following outlined items below. Learning to save and be cost effective at the same time is your number one goal. You can see all 195 countries if you like, using strategies to budget properly.

The next guideline in *ULTIMATE EXPERIENCE* is to be frugal and save your money wisely. And, I'll add, invest wisely in things that will have a return on your investment. Saving really is about being habitual with your hard-earned money. Be disciplined and aware of your spending. Eliminate the unnecessary wasted spending to achieve your dream of seeing the world!

Traveling is obtainable for all those who desire it. A common misconception is that it costs a fortune and that you must have a loaded bank account to be able to travel. Most would be surprised to learn how much a trip across the globe could cost if it is planned out right. The biggest expense during a vacation is usually the flights followed by accommodation.

Flights can drain your budget quickly. But accruing travel points flying, following up on airline deals, and being an airline rewards member, might offset some of those costs. And sometimes, you will see travel deals for flights or better rates if you book in advance.

Accommodation is the second cost that can drop your bank account balance. Like the airlines, try to accrue points as a hotel rewards member. Research off season deals, off the map locations, and giveaways for staying during a slow part of the year. When it comes to lodging, there are numerous options, which include hotels, hostels, room rentals, Airbnb, and campsites, amongst others. You can opt for whichever suits you best and fits your budget. As with flights, booking in

Cappadocia, Turkey

advance or watching for a cancellation may save you hundreds or even thousands per trip.

Now I will caution one warning with hotels, especially in some countries where it's a little shady, and the U.S. is not exempt from these. Some places have been known to give one rate, and check you in at that rate. Then three days later, when you have had the time of your life, they throw in on your way out, a fifty-dollar hospitality fee here or an additional room fee in there. Yes, it can be quite upsetting. My advice again, do your research and read the fine print.

Once the matters of flight and lodging are sorted, the rest of the travel planning is rather easy to devise. You've picked the best airline, at a great rate or free if you hit those free flight flyer miles in your travels. The same for the luxurious hotel which you got for next to nothing being the hotel's rewards member too. Or was it the scheduling of reservations months in advance that did the trick? Maybe, all the above. As a new traveler, that might not be applicable to you yet….. but it will (speaking it into existence for you).

Let's get real about maximizing the money for the trip. This will be the tough love section. If your heart is really into travel, and you want to get all you can out of the experience, there'll be some work to do. Saving for a trip will require some needed discipline on your part. That means getting rid of some of your wasteful spending and doing away with unnecessary things. Let's dive into my travel budget philosophy further.

THE ULTIMATE EXPERIENCE

1. **Plan.** Plan ahead months or even years in advance, if necessary.
2. **Save.** Save, Save, Save and then save some more.
3. **Execute.** Put the planning and money together. It's time to get things moving.

Remember:
Every day you put off travel you miss out on an experience.

Now, let's cut to the chase. We spend more on our hair, nails, wardrobe, food addictions, going out and extracurricular activities than any vacation will ever cost. Being from Los Angeles, I find food and restaurants comparatively reasonable when I visit other countries than in the U.S. Not even kidding, the cost of an average weekend hanging out in my city is equivalent to the cost of an entire trip to South America. So, it is up to you to make up your mind about what you are willing to sacrifice if you truly want to see the world.

Before I was financially secure, my desire to travel was fulfilled by budgeting. Everything I ate, wore, and purchased, was based on my goal of saving money so that I had enough to spare for travel. I always understood that money returns, but time doesn't. I also knew going to school, building a stable career and life for myself would all pay off one day. The reward would be my ability to afford all the basic necessities along with the luxuries of life, which, to me, has always included traveling. With that thought in mind, I gave it my all until I was able to reach that stage in life.

Frankly speaking, when I was financially unstable and had a tight budget, I stopped eating out and went to extreme lengths to save. I resorted to eating Top Ramen noodles which cost me 25 cents per meal (this was in my college days). Getting my hair done was never an added cost, because I always did it myself. In regards to my wardrobe, I have never been brand conscious; wearing brand names was not an accomplishment in my eyes. I shopped at The Alley in downtown LA or Forever 21 and got dressed at a very reasonable price. And believe me when I tell you, despite not spending that much, I still looked like a million bucks because it wasn't on me; it was in me (just like it's in you too!). To keep it a buck, I still budget regardless of how much I make. If you want to save money on your wardrobe, check out Shein.com…. outfits are cheap as hell and you will still look amazing.

Budgeting essentially means having control of your spending habits. It is all about understanding and prioritizing your needs, utilizing your existing resources, and using what you have to get what you want. The problem with people these days is their willingness to override their needs for their wants, which is an unhealthy and irrational practice. Always prioritize and have patience with yourself. When you are on a mission to greatness, putting good in the atmosphere, striving to achieve success, and doing your best, the universe will eventually give you the desires of your heart. Having faith, but never making any efforts for what you want would never lead you anywhere. It's imperative that you put in the work.

If you are patiently waiting to get "flewed out," then you just might end up waiting your whole life, or even worse… get flown out and have the worst experience of your life. If you aren't hip and don't know what 'flewed out' is…. is just slang for a sugar daddy or sugar momma to take you on a trip for free! I've heard horror stories of people going on a trip out of the country with someone who paid for everything and ended up stranded due to a disagreement or not performing a sexual favor. As a woman, being invited on a trip with a man by all means allow him to be the man and pay… but have enough money to take care of yourself if things were to go left. I encourage you to take charge, even if that means getting you an additional job or hobby that can generate money.

I'm good at budgeting, but when it came down to it, I had to get an additional job to maintain my needs and wants without having to worry or depend on anyone else. My primary job takes care of my mortgage, insurance policies, food, bills, and car notes. My secondary jobs fund my extracurricular activities like fancy dining, shopping, saving, and severe travel addiction. My third job and my business is just passive income that goes to my nonprofit organization and additional savings. Maintaining a

second and third job is not always realistic for everyone, which is totally understandable. However, simple budgeting will do the trick, even if it allows you to afford only one trip a year. And honestly, something is better than nothing. We all need an escape from our daily routine and a hard reset in order to rebalance. My trips give me something to always look forward to.

My best advice is to save, save, and save some more. You will be so surprised at how much money you can save by not eating out all the time, going a few months without getting your nails done, watching YouTube to learn how to do hair so you can do your own, skip going out on the weekends, etc. Don't laugh at me, but…. You can still catch me in a thrift store near you. I'm sure you still laughed… and that's cool!! Even though I make six figures a year, every penny counts in my book. Never in a million years had I thought about thrifting until I followed this dope chick on Instagram @thriftntell (true fashion diva), which gave me the inspiration to start. I don't go thrifting very often, but when I do go, I come up with some serious looks. A lot of stuff in thrift stores is brand spanking new (for the bougie people in the back), so don't cheat yourself…. treat yourself. Now, if you aren't interested in going to those lengths, I understand. But I'm just trying to let you know there's various ways to save your coins.

We really don't realize how much money we spend in our daily lives. If experiencing travel is something you really want to do, I encourage you wholeheartedly. The biggest expense is the flight and the hotel accommodation as I mentioned earlier. Nowadays, there are even layaways for flights, which I have never tried. But it's a really good option. Regarding lodging accommodation, there are options for every budget.

Figure 9: Table of basic Travel Expenses.

Transportation	45%
Accommodation	25%
Food	15%
Activities	10%
Other (Shopping, etc.)	5%

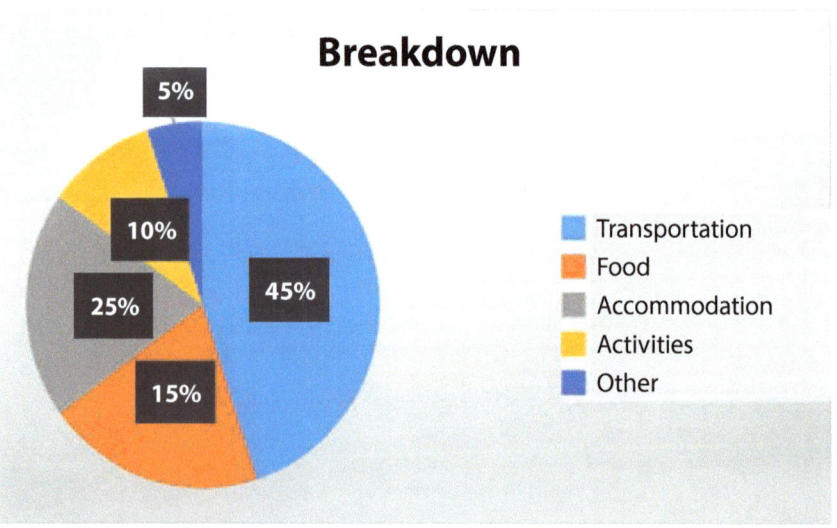

Figure 10: Pie Chart of Expenses. Comparison of overall costs. This can vary depending on the time of the year and destination.

SAVINGS CHECKLIST

1. Stop eating at restaurants. Besides, you will do a better and safer job handling your own food. Not to mention, it's a healthier benefit to consume home-cooked meals.
2. Buy your housing supplies—toiletries, disinfectants, and cleaners, wholesale online or at a bulk supply. A few good examples are Costco, Amazon and Sam's Club.
3. Check the stores, magazines, online, and newspapers for sales and coupons.
4. If you are a woman, do your own manicure and pedicure. If you are addicted to having long nails, get you some good looking press-ons for heaven's sake.
5. Do your own hair sis! If hair is just really not a skill you can master, have a friend learn and do it for you. YouTube is the best place to get detailed tutorials and turn you into a beauty guru.
6. For my fellas… y'all don't have as many extracurricular expenses in regards to beauty, so you are already in the lead toward savings!

NOTE: Just do these few simple steps and you'll be amazed how much money you will save for so many travel trips.

Managing your budget is indeed a very crucial part of planning a trip. People tend to go overboard and overspend while traveling. With a proper budget in place, you can avoid making that mistake. Regardless of the destination and duration of your trip, you need to have a properly planned budget. It is important to list all your expenses and manage your budget smartly.

Never sacrifice your rent and bill money to go on a trip or even during a trip. I cannot stress how important it is to prioritize and be responsible. I have seen so many people go way over their budget and come home flat broke. Please don't do that to yourself. Live within your means, beloved. Plan, save and then execute!

Conclusion

Let's recap what we learned. A budget is a great tool to help you travel the world. Budgeting and saving helps to minimize costs to have the necessary money you'll need on your vacation. Learning to save, and be cost effective at the same time is your number one goal. You can see the world for yourself if you adopt budgeting strategies, remove wasteful spending on unnecessary items, and find ways to cut down your expenses.

If you can start saving money by budgeting and cutting unnecessary consumption costs— the world is yours! Traveling is truly attainable for all those who desire it. There's a million and one ways to make money, but you have to know how to manage it when you make it. Honestly, if you keep working hard to be successful in life, sooner than later you won't even have to worry about strictly saving and budgeting.

Remember again, a common misconception is that it costs a fortune and that you have to have a loaded bank account to be able to travel. Most would be surprised to learn how much a trip across the globe could cost if it is planned out right. The biggest expense during a vacation is usually the flights followed by the accommodations. Be mindful to research the flights and accommodations carefully to avoid unnecessary costs, hidden fees, and/or overpricing. A little research will save you a lot.

We've gone through our strategies to save you thousands of dollars for your future adventure. I have shared with you the tools necessary to not only save but earn additional income to travel. Where do we go from here with all that money?

Porto Novo, Benin

Let's go forward and explore a not-so exciting but necessary experience. We're going to discuss the pros, and cons of the process in reaching our destination that we all go through traveling. I promise to give you great advice, and tips to make the process less problematic.

CHAPTER 5:

It's Not the Journey, It's the Destination

Stop worrying about the potholes in the road and enjoy the trip. — ***Babs Hoffman***

Don't let the airport, train, bus, or cruise ship experience be the reason you don't travel. Yes, it can be very stressful, and is my least favorite part of the travel experience. The TSA checkpoints alone are nerve wracking. Putting everything you are carrying in a small security basket that never fits all your stuff can be a challenge in itself. Having to take off your shoes and walk on a floor full of germs of all sorts to go through a metal detector is something that can be abominable to perceive. To even think of you having no socks and having to walk barefoot… adds insult to injury and disgust. But remember when it comes to travel.. It's not the journey, it's the destination.

Let's go over the various means of travel—planes, boats, trains, and some tips to make everything a smooth process.

Airport Flights

Try to avoid flight connections that are very short, which for me is anything that's less than 2 hours. I have had an international flight that was late departing, which resulted in the plane arriving late and I missed my connecting flight. Nothing is worse than running through an airport trying to board a flight and get to the gate to discover that the doors are closed and the vessel is backing away from the gate. Now you are stuck in a foreign country for the night. In cases where you missed your flight due to the fault of an airline, request them to compensate you for the inconvenience with a hotel, food voucher and reschedule of the next available flight. Definitely hold them accountable. All in all, be proactive and give yourself time, at least 2 hours.

Second, make sure you get there early enough for check-in. Most likely, there will be traffic, long lines and congested security checkpoints before you even get to reach the check-in counter. All airlines close checked luggage one hour before departure, no exceptions! So even if you arrive an hour prior… and you have not made it to your terminal and at the check-in counter by that time, expect to miss your flight.

Be sure to have your passport and boarding ticket readily available, but still very secure. Going through various checkpoints, it is easy to mishandle and lose your vital documents, so be very mindful. I usually wear a crossbody bag and always keep my passport and money in front of me on my chest.

Yes, it is mandatory to take off your shoes, so wear easily removable shoes and socks so you don't have to walk barefoot. The limit for any liquid is 4oz. Anything over 4 ounces, you need to put in your check-in luggage or breakdown into toiletry size containers (you can find them at the dollar store). If you forget and take your large perfume bottle or lotions with you to the TSA checkpoint, just know it will be thrown away no matter the cost. Be proactive and check your bags for any water or fluids to make sure you go through with no problems, especially when you are already running late and on the verge of missing your flight. Large devices like iPads and laptops have to be taken out of your bag and placed in a separate bin. It can definitely be a hassle getting through security, but if you are prepared and follow directions, it will be so much smoother of a process.

Once you have made it through security, don't wander around the airport as if you can't get left. Imagine losing track of time, going to an airport restaurant and ending up missing your flight. Please believe that passengers do it all the time. Nothing drives an airline company crazier than having to wait on delayed passengers, which most won't. Now, to think of it, it drives the passengers bonkers, too. Always be mindful of your time.

Try to travel light in the airport so that you can be comfortable. Dress in layers so you won't be cold and whenever you get hot, you can just simply remove one layer at a time. I always carry my medication, headphones, compression socks, pen, passport/money/cards, charger cords, laptop, neck pillow and phone with me on the plane in my personal bag. Depending on how long my stay is, I will have everything in my carry on. My packing cubes allow me to get a lot more into my carry-on luggage because it compresses so well. My preference is a carry-on versus checked luggage because it saves me money, I don't have to worry about it getting lost, and upon arrival at my destination I don't have to wait at the carousel for my luggage to drop.

Fear of Flying

Many people don't travel because of their fear of flying. The medical terminology for that is *aviophobia*. Aviophobia is intense fear or dislike of flying, and should be addressed appropriately before attempting to take a flight. Factors that contribute to this phobia is fear of heights, claustrophobia, turbulence, etc. If that happens to be you, I want to provide you with some statistical data that may put your mind at ease.

Your odds of being in an accident during a flight is 1 in 1.2 million, and the chances of that accident being fatal are 1 in 11

million. Moreover, your chances of dying in a car crash, conversely, are 1 in 5,000 (simplefly, 2022). Knowing facts about the odds still won't eliminate the fear completely, so let's talk about some remedies that will help you cope better on your flight.

1. Do not consume caffeine before your flight. Caffeine further contributes to jitteriness, which is what you do not need if you are already anxious.

2. Contact your doctor for a prescription to decrease your anxiety and panic. Medications like Xanax or Valium can be prescribed by your physician to help you stay calm.

3. Try to get some rest on the flight. I usually board my flight very tired, so I can sleep. The best feeling is sleeping the entire duration of the flight and waking up upon arrival.

4. Keep yourself distracted. If you are the person who will never be able to sleep on a flight, then keep yourself entertained. Watching a movie, listening to music, reading a book, or playing a game, will keep you occupied.

5. Accept the fact that there will most likely be turbulence. Turbulence is a part of the flight experience, which causes planes to suddenly jolt and shake while in the air. It is considered a fairly normal occurrence and nothing to fear. Just think of turbulence as a pothole in the sky!

6. Try breathing exercises and meditation before boarding to keep your nerves calm.

7. Sit in the aisle seat. Especially if you have a fear of heights, stay away from the window.

8. Alert the flight attendant that you have a fear of flying. Some flight attendants are really friendly and have experience with passengers with the same situation.

My advice would be to start off slowly by taking a short (one to two hour) flight first utilizing some of the tips I gave you, and see how you do. If you do well… which I know you will, then start going longer distances. I hope some of these techniques help you get past your fear so you can start to explore the world!

Sailing Ships

Arrive early for boarding a vessel. Sometimes customs and passport checks take a little longer than expected for ships. If you have a history of motion sickness or have never been on a boat and don't know if you will get motion sickness, I suggest getting medication just in case (Dramamine can be purchased over the counter at your local drug store). Believe it or not, I have never been on a cruise ship! Cruises are not my thing, but I did put it on my to-do list this year.

Trains

Trains can provide a unique and nostalgic experience for those who hate to fly. Especially, when you ride across several countries

Wadi Rum, Jordan

with various beautiful landscapes. If it's self-seating, get there early so you can get a window seat for the views. Now, if you can reserve seating, I would advise that you pay extra for a window seat. Preferably as far away from the restroom as possible for the sake of traffic and of not riding the whole trip smelling urine and feces. As with all modes of travel, arrive early for boarding so that you won't get left.

Buses

The same principle in regards to early arrival applies to taking a bus as your mode of transportation. Be mindful that it is the cheapest, but also takes the longest to reach the destination. It is said that the safest seats on a bus are in the middle. Bring snacks, because unlike a plane or a train ride, there will be no attendants handing out food or drinks. Once your luggage is under the bus (stored), you will not be able to retrieve it until you reach your destination. Take a book, headphones, pillow, blanket, and a toiletry bag. Try to choose an overnight bus trip so you can get some rest.

Here's a few pro tips that are highly advised:

PRO TIP 1:

Download apps for vessel, train, and flight updates. These apps are great at getting information to you in real time. Especially when it involves any sudden changes. When you have the app downloaded and you are signed in, you get instant updates, arrival, departures, and specific transit information. Make sure your notifications are on so you do not miss the latest travel information. Always make a profile with the application so that you can accumulate points/rewards and have a hassle-free log in.

PRO TIP 2:

Check into your flight or train as soon as possible. Security, check-in, and baggage drop offs take time to facilitate. Delays can cause you to miss your respective mode of transportation. For most international travelers, you will not be able to check-in through the app because you have to show your passport at the ticket counter. When traveling internationally, please arrive at least 2 to 3 hours ahead of your departure (not including the time it takes to get there). Don't leave your accommodation 2 hours ahead of time, actually be inside the airport at least 2 hours prior to your departure time!

PRO TIP 3:

Pay for bags in advance to save time and money. Bags are always cheaper to add to your flight when you purchase them ahead of time. At the counter, it's usually chaotic and hectic for the travel workers. So don't take it personal when they don't possess the most cheerful demeanor or are as helpful as you feel they should be. Nowadays, there are self-check-in machines at most airports and you have to print out your own luggage tag and boarding pass. So don't be shocked if you arrive and can only talk to an agent once you have first visited a machine.

> **PRO TIP 4:**
>
> Dress comfortably, including easily removable shoes. Most train trips and flights are very cold. Dressing in layers can be a huge lifesaver. To prevent restless leg syndrome, leg swelling and possible formation of blood clots (which can be life threatening), I wear compression socks. Walk around if you can to keep circulation flowing to your legs. A lot of people don't know that sitting for extended hours can take a toll on your lower extremities (aka legs), because gravity pulls your blood down and reduces circulation. Compression socks work by applying gentle pressure to your leg muscles, veins, arteries, and tissues to support the blood traveling back to the heart. Not trying to give you an anatomy course, but I'm a nurse first and education is power!!!! To purchase comfortable high quality compression socks, head over to my online travel accessories store at www.morlife.shop

Conclusion

To recap, don't let the airport, train station, or bus ride experience overwhelm you and be the reason you don't travel. Yes, it can be very stressful, and it is my least favorite part of the travel experience but it's all a part of the process. If you have a fear of flying, start off taking a short flight implementing the remedies that I shared with you. If you can tolerate the airplane ride, then I think you can challenge yourself to go further and further.

So, you've learned the best tips for flying by plane, traveling by boat, bus and even a train. You're ready to get out there and see that incredible world of ours. What could possibly slow you down?

What happens when you run out of money on a trip? You know the fee they tell you about four days into the trip after you have had the time of your life. What can you possibly do to remedy the situation when the funds are unexpectedly gone in the middle of the trip?

Fellow traveler, no worries. There's a plan in the next chapter to get you through this minor obstacle. Read on.

CHAPTER 6:

All About the Money

You don't have to be rich to travel well. – **Eugene Fodor**

You planned out the trip. You reviewed all the airlines, looked into all the recent data of the country you want to visit such as language, customs, food, currency rates for your money, etc. But you went even further, and followed up with the U.S. Embassy and Council on Foreign Relations advisories online. You meticulously saved every penny for this trip. Wait, you actually made some money….. You were not playing, were you? Now, you have a bonus wad of cash! Where do we go from here?

Additional money and emergency funds will be needed on the journey. Now we will use both to execute our plan to be safe and not over spend. Overspending on a trip has been fraught with many pitfalls for travelers. With that said, we need to fine tune our execution of the *Ultimate Experience.*

1. The Dangers of Running out of Money

Running out of money while traveling can be dangerous. The majority of people do not set a budget when they are traveling. In my case, it is the complete opposite. To stay stress-free throughout my trip, I tend to make a checklist of each of my expenses and plan a budget ahead of time. The budget can include accommodation expenses, food, and souvenirs. This way, I never find myself in a dreadful situation of running out of money while traveling. Likewise, it is also essential to return from a trip without the guilt of having overspent. Thus, making a budget and keeping a checklist of items accordingly will prove to be a lifesaver!

2. Carrying Money

I always carry cash with me for food, souvenirs, tours, shopping, and tips. However, the extra money that is outside of my projected spending amount, I carry in the form of a debit or credit card. To be completely honest, I always have both. The reason I carry a credit card and debit card is because not every place accepts credit cards. And some countries won't accept the dollar (Brazil or Turkey will certainly want you to use their currency.) Then there is the joy of using an ATM in another language with no one around to help you decipher the machine… clearly I'm just being sarcastic.

The reason why I carry my debit card is because I can retrieve money from the ATM if need be. Cash is king in most foreign countries, especially in rural areas. Knowing your money's value in each respective country is important too. For example, in Africa, the rate of the dollar is usually way higher than the local money. But in the Middle East or England, if you try to impress them with a dollar these days, they'll laugh you out of their country.

PRO TIP:

Download a Currency Calculator app on your phone. The one I use is Currency Converter Plus. It comes in handy because when I am shopping and they tell me a price, I pull out my converter and make sure I'm not being bamboozled... and most times once I do the calculation, I am. Being a foreigner and a woman, some people try to take advantage and overcharge, but not on my watch! Don't fall victim to being overcharged.

3. Credit Cards

Credit cards are not a bad thing, if you use them to your advantage. Not only do they help build credit history, but they are safe and secure. There are many pros to having a credit card such as cash back, rewards points, universal acceptance, convenience, recordkeeping, amongst other things. The cons are high interest rates, fees, and temptation to spend money that you don't have. For me, I use credit cards to my benefit and maximize the pros.

The number one rule is to only use the credit card if you have the money to pay it back in full. The exception to that would be an emergency situation and you have no other choice. In the case of utilizing credit when you don't have the means of paying it back in full, it is mandatory and vitally important that you at least make the minimum payment on time.

The worst thing you can do to your financial health is mess up your credit. I have many credit cards, roughly about 30 active currently. I use them to show activity, but I pay for them in full each statement. In the past when I did not have a sufficient amount of funds, sometimes I had to resort to using my credit cards for survival. However, during those difficult times I always stayed below 30% utilization of my available credit. What that means is if you have $10,000 of available credit (no matter how many cards make up that amount), you want to only utilize less than $3,000. Nonetheless, my hope for you is to have abundance in every area of your life and never have to utilize a credit card for any purpose but to put yourself at a higher credit score.

Platinum AMEX: the Ultimate travel credit card

My all-time favorite credit card for travel purposes is the Platinum American Express Card. The perks

of the Platinum AMEX card is also having access to the American Express Global Lounge Collection, with more than 1,400 airport lounges across 650 cities in over 140 countries. Whenever I have a layover, I'm without stress due to having access to lounges with food, drinks, Wi-Fi, sometimes even showers and a spa.

Have you ever heard of CLEAR? Clear is a new system that is used in the airport, that uses biometrics to identify you, which allows you to move faster through security at select airports and stadiums across the US… and the membership is covered through the platinum card.

Still not impressed? Okay…. You can earn points up to five times on flights, five times on prepaid hotels, and one time on other purchases. Not to mention $200 Hotel Credit each year on select prepaid hotel bookings and $200 Airline Fee Credit per calendar year when incidental travel fees on qualifying airlines are charged. It's even more perks that I haven't even mentioned, but these are my favorites that are applicable to traveling. Let's just say, the Platinum AMEX card has amazing benefits for travelers, both novice and expert travelers. The annual fee is currently $695 a year, but it's worth it to me.

True Story:

I was new to international traveling and really excited to be done with my Master's degree program. For the first time in my life, I had the freedom, both financially and physically, so I picked a destination trip to India, Sri Lanka and Maldives (all in one trip). I asked my childhood friend Nychelle who also graduated from the same Nursing program to come with me on the trip, and she agreed. We were both already working as nurses, we were without any responsibilities, and we thought we were ballin' (rich). She didn't ask any questions or details because she knew I loved planning trips, and I was going to have us doing something fun yet luxurious. I calculated the flights and hotel accommodations; she sent her portion and WE were READY TO GO.

We boarded our flight in Los Angeles to San Francisco which was our layover location before we went to India. We got to San Francisco and chilled a little while before boarding our flight for INDIA, and then…. The lady at the ticketing counter asked us for our visas. Immediately I felt impending doom because I had done all of this research for our trip and didn't check if we needed a damn visa. I was so sorry to myself, but most importantly to my friend for taking this journey with me and I didn't even let her know we needed a visa. I kept my composure and luckily my friend was not upset with me. Long story short, we got our bags off the plane and sat down in the airport lobby to strategize. I found an emergency visa service company in India whose turnaround was 24 hours. We both paid about $120 each for the visa.

The catch is that we had to purchase new flights and get a hotel for the night in San Francisco. However, I volunteered to purchase our ticket from San Fran to India because it was my fault we were in this position. Luckily, I had the 'emergency funds' to do it. It was an invaluable lesson though. We were one-day late arriving in India, so we lost a day of touring and a night of hotel costs. Rule number one, is do your RESEARCH! Even when you research the country, dig deeper and research the entry requirements. I also learned that many airports have an emergency visa station for such cases.

PRO TIP:

For all travel accommodations expenses, I use my Platinum American Express Card for the purpose of collecting points. To give you a gem, I use my Platinum AMEX card like it's my debit card, and pay it off completely every statement to avoid interest. Not only does that boost my credit and show activity, but every dollar spent gives me points which can be used toward future travel.

4. Emergency Funds

It is important to always have extra money in case of an emergency. When I say an emergency, it's not always the end of the world, so don't panic! It could be something as little as needing to purchase a new hotel for the night, or as big as missing your flight due to oversleeping and now you need to purchase a whole new plane ticket.

In Travel Money Checklist

- Keep emergency funds on you when you travel (it can be in the form of a card, which is my preference). If you lose a card, you can simply call your bank and cancel it. If you lose money, there is no getting it back.
- Keep the emergency money safe and out of sight of would-be thieves.
- Know the U.S. dollar currency rates of the country you are visiting. Remember some countries prize the dollar. Others…not so much.
- Always prepare for an unforeseen delay, extra possible flight, or additional room in the event of an extended layover. Flights have been known to get delayed, logistics get messed up, and travel coordinators make mistakes.
- Money is not the same everywhere.

Research is key when it comes to visiting any place for the first time. Almost every country I've visited accepts US currency. The US dollar is powerful. However, I've visited some countries that could care less about the US dollar. They only want their currency. That was true in other countries such as Turkey, India, areas of England. These countries I know accept US dollars, but sometimes they can give you a hassle about it. At any rate, I retrieve the amount I plan to spend at home so I can avoid paying extra ATM and bank fees. To give you an example, El Salvador no longer uses their native currency and has adopted US dollar only. In the interim, if I know the US dollar is worthless then I do not bring US currency and get my money at the ATM or bank. Just know what is applicable. Knowledge is really power.

Conclusion

Execute the plan by having your back up savings and strategies ready. Have back up money on you hidden or secured safely away. Also keep your debit and credit card handy as another resource back up. Make sure you research the value of your money traveling to any location. Nothing is more frustrating than not getting your dollar's value on a vacation. Return from your trip without the guilt of overspending and getting your money's worth!

It can be dangerous to run out of money while traveling. The majority of people do not set a budget or account for surprise costs when they are traveling. Stay stress-free during your trip and use my advice for budgeting, pro tips, and the checklist.

So, we have learned what to do when you get that unforeseen additional charge. You have kept your back up money and cards safely secured and ready. You followed the travel checklists and pro tips. You are making a tremendous and memorable voyage. What's next to explore on travels? Safe, safely, safest!

CHAPTER 7:

Get Back Home Safe

A ship in a harbor is safe, but that is not what ships are built for.
— ***John A. Shedd***

The number one goal is to always be safe.

No words can express how grateful I am to have traveled all over the world and returned home safely each time. Before, during, and after my trips, I thank God for traveling grace. I always trust that I will experience the world and all its beauty with the help of his guidance and the universe navigating my steps. However, I do believe that faith without work is dead… meaning that I must make safe decisions while traveling, especially as a solo black woman.

Altun Ha Maya Ruins, Belize

I will share some of my greatest safety tips in this chapter.

We continue to follow our guidelines for THE ULTIMATE EXPERIENCE. This all started back in the planning phases of your trip months or years ago. We put this return home plan together most likely at the same time we planned out the trip. Now, as we implement it, we have to stay alert and not get distracted on our journey.

1. Location Safety

Never share your current location in REAL TIME. For example, posting a picture with the location tagged is a big No-No! However, it's more than okay to post and tag the location once you have left. Many people do LIVE videos and generally want to share the moment with followers, family and friends back home, but that's also risky. Be mindful while you are posting a video or doing a live on social media, which includes having visible signs of the location in your pictures and videos. You will be surprised how many stalkers there are in the world, not to mention robbers and rapists. Literally, there are people that look up locations by way of hashtag locations of users that are actively using or have used that location. And they've advanced to using Artificial Intelligence (AI) and Search Engine Optimization (SEO) software to increase their chances of finding victims.

> **PRO TIP:**
>
> If you are in another country and don't want to be tracked by your phone or devices, get temporary phones, burner systems, or VPN's (virtual private network) to protect yourself. A way to turn off your location temporarily is by turning on airplane mode. Another option is to stop sharing your location with all apps and services on your iPhone, for any given time. To do that, go to Settings > Privacy > Location Services and turn off location sharing. For android, open your Setting > Personal > Location access > at the top of the screen, turn Access to my location off. I honestly do not turn off my location when I'm traveling. However, I just wanted to share with you that there's options if you are concerned about it.

2. Solo Safety Advice

Never casually tell strangers that you are alone. They could use that as an opportunity to take advantage. I don't engage in nightlife such as clubs or bars and during the day I travel with intention when I am on a solo trip. What I mean by that is, I always have an itinerary for my days planned out. Touring with a guide has never failed me. In rare cases that I explore by myself, I am always aware of my surroundings, and I know exactly where my destination is (i.e., nearby restaurant, coffee house, activity). I ensure that I get international wireless connection through my phone carrier. Initially, I had AT&T, but I switched to T-Mobile because it has better international rates which save me hundreds of dollars annually.

3. Appearances Should Be Deceiving

Be mindful of your appearance. A crook is always looking for an opportunity to find someone with money. Flaunting your clothing, expensive shoes, designer purses, money, credit cards, or jewelry, in front of a seasoned criminal, you are running the risk of being robbed. Check out the U. S. Embassy crime statistics if you don't believe me.

True Story:

I made the mistake of bringing my diamond rings on vacation with me. We had daily cleaning service (2 to 3 maids per day), and one of the maids took one of my rings and left the others while I was in Turks and Caicos staying at Neptune Villas. I took it off and put it in my jewelry box the day before I was leaving to travel back home. I knew I had my jewelry box and when I looked in it, all my gold jewelry seemed to be there but I didn't count them. Once I made it to Miami for an extended layover, I realized that my most expensive ring was gone and reported it to the hotel manager via telephone. But, because I was already gone and didn't have evidence, they didn't do anything. This was my lesson to never take expensive jewelry on another vacation. In other cases, you don't want to put yourself in a position of being a target and get robbed.

4. Be Modest

How you dress is important and how you represent yourself is likely how you will be approached. It is fine to dress as revealing as you please, but nine times out of ten will get attention you do not want. In my experience as a solo black female, I get enough attention just based on my skin color and textured hair alone. In many countries that I have been to, black tourists are a rarity and don't happen every day. So YES, you will stand out if you are of color. With that being said, don't call any unwanted attention to yourself… unless that's your goal.

There is definitely an hyper-sexualization of black women in the media on all platforms. Across the globe, women of all races are demeaned and dehumanized as objects. However, black women are the most unprotected and disrespected. I read once in an article that we are either ignored or fetishized over, and I agree. There are so many racial biases that pose safety risks and concerns that are valid. Which is a very harsh reality that I take into consideration because I am a black woman. Moreover, I travel with integrity, caution, consciousness and understanding. No matter your race or ethnicity, represent yourself well, stay conscious and please stay safe.

Awareness and knowledge are extremely important. Dress appropriate to the situation and occasion at hand. If you are at the beach or pool of course a swimsuit is appropriate. However,

Abu Dhabi, United Emirates

True Story:

Me and my friend were visiting the Sheikh Zayed Grand Mosque in Abu Dhabi. We knew that there was a strict dress code and that we needed to be properly covered in order to enter. We took a trip to the mall and brought beautiful long dresses all the way down to the floor, thinking we were going to be looking appropriate, yet fly at the same time. We got up the next morning and had our tour guide drive us from Dubai to Abu Dhabi.

When we got to Abu Dhabi, he said "You have to change now."

Our reply was "Change for what?"

He explained to us that our forearms were showing and that was prohibited. Being a local tour guide, he was able to rent us clothing with hijabs in the parking lot of the mosque (which was illegal). We could've gone to jail for not following the rules of the mosque. In some religious countries, there are rules and customs that must be followed. As foreigners and tourists, entering the country in total ignorance of culture, laws, and customs, you open yourself up for incidents that could lead you to trouble. The kind of problems—a fine or jail, which could make your experience the ultimate disaster. Therefore, know the laws, the customs, the culture, and any nuances to keep yourself safe!

if you are visiting a Buddhist temple in a country like Bali, you will have to follow the dress code.

5. Stay Woke (SITUATIONAL AWARENESS)

There's nothing wrong with drinking, but please drink responsibly. Sometimes when we drink, we go overboard, and past our limitations. This is when you become vulnerable and do things that you wouldn't do if you were in a sober state. I'm not a big drinker and just started casually drinking in my 30's. I refrain from drinking while I am on a solo trip, unless I am at my hotel or accompanied by someone I know. Even one drink could alter my judgment, so I am usually very cautious.

If drinking is your thing, do not leave your drink unattended (rather alcoholic or non-alcoholic). There are many cases around the world where people have been drugged by strangers putting powder substances and pills in their drinks while they are not looking. Even if you make "friends"… don't trust friendly strangers! There are stories of people who disguise themselves as fellow travelers and they are actually natives looking for potential people to befriend and set up. I'm not here to scare you, I just want you to be on your 10 toes at all times.

6. Safe accommodations

Choose lodging accommodation that has a front desk and preferably security. I do not stay in hostels, specifically for safety and privacy reasons. However, if hostels are your preference due

Capernaum, Israel

to saving money, please be sure to choose one that has proper security measures in place.

Above all, my hope and prayer for EVERY traveler is to never encounter danger or be put in harm's way. No doubt bad things can happen regardless of how cautious or safe one plays it, but the more cautious the better. My outlook on traveling is; I have been safer overseas than some of my loved ones were at home. You really can't go through life living in fear, because it will paralyze your very existence.

My best advice is to be aware of your environment and move accordingly.

Checklist to Get Home Safe

- Make sure to let family and friends know where you are going. I usually type up my entire itinerary and share it with my emergency contact via email or text.
- Never share your current location when traveling on any application—laptop, phone, iPad, etc. unless it is your loved ones.
- Do not tag yourself in your current location on social media in REAL TIME (YouTube, Facebook, Twitter, Instagram, etc.).
- You should travel with someone but if you do go it alone (like I do), do not tell strangers you are traveling alone.
- Be mindful of your appearance. Don't dress overly provocative. You really don't want to get uncomfortable stares and unwanted attention while traveling.

- Flashy, expensive jewelry should stay out of sight—locked up in the hotel's private safe or left at home. Again, thieves and kidnappers can spot a high dollar target easily when you shine too brightly with jewelry.
- If you drink alcohol, watch your drinking during your travels. Impaired judgment in a remote destination can be a recipe for disaster.
- Monitor your drinks and anything you eat or intake—including food and medication.
- Choose lodgings that have good security and a twenty-four-hour front desk.

Conclusion

There are an infinite number of words that will never cover how extremely grateful I have been to travel, to see, and to feel various experiences all over the world. Also, to immerse myself in such emotional bliss and then return home safely. Before my trip I bring all the good vibrations I can. During the trip—overwhelmed by the exotic destinations, tantalized by the mysteriousness during my adventure, and fervidly complete after my trips, I speak positively over my journey. In my dreams and in my recollections, I envision myself dancing in a firelit cove, hearing the sway of a desert wind, or some other lasting adventure before I even leave home. Many times, what I dream about always surpasses my expectations. God—infinite in his expanse across the cosmos, always navigates my steps along the way. Under his guidance, I always trust that I will experience the world grounded and surrounded in all its radiant beauty. However, especially journeying home, I do believe that faith without work is dead… meaning that I have to make safe decisions while traveling, especially as a solo black woman.

I have shared some of my greatest safety tips in this chapter to help you plan the journey home.

So, where are we now on our journey, fellow traveler? You meticulously planned and saved your money. You sat down, and planned every step of your journey there and back. You may have gone so far as to plan for things while you were there, too. You have your money saved for the trip and any unknown expenses. And more importantly you have gone over the safety techniques. What's our next plan? How do we communicate with the different people we meet on our journeys? Are there a few common phrases to help us until our guide shows up to interpret?

Let's explore a few of these in the next chapter.

CHAPTER 8:

Communication is Key

We should learn languages because language is the only thing worth knowing even poorly. — ***Kato Lomb***

Being able to communicate effectively with other people is essential. In most countries around the world, English is spoken even if it's minimal. I usually try to learn the basic courtesy words like Hello, Thank you, etc., of the country which I will be visiting. Because I am intrigued with culture, I usually visit rural areas where English is not common. In cases such as this, I hire a guide that speaks the native language of the people. Under THE ULTIMATE EXPERIENCE, this falls into the planning of our trip.

Definitely, I encourage you to have a guide on hand who does speak the language of the area you are visiting. Do not make the mistake of assuming everyone in the world speaks English.

Many of the places I explored did not speak English. Identify the keys to effective communication—the language, the customs, the culture, and the country's laws, before the trip starts.

I cannot emphasize this point enough. You want to avoid incidents or trouble caused by a lack of understanding and communication. You should know the language so you can hire a guide who would know the specific laws, the customs, the culture, socio-political systems, and even the religion in some cases, to be fully aware of the place you will be exploring.

Of course I am NOT telling you that you need to learn a whole new language just to visit a country for the first and probably only time (that would be insane). What I am suggesting is, if you plan to visit a rural area, a tribe, etc., you can always hire a guide and/or interpreter for translation. This needs to be added to the travel plans in advance. And part of avoiding an embarrassing situation or worse, is communicating effectively. I utilize Google translate a lot when traveling abroad (if I have decent enough service), when I am without a guide. Part of being alert on your journey is knowing what people may be saying or asking you.

PRO TIP:

There is an app called "Private Guide", which is my go to if I am seeking a guide native to the country I will be visiting. In each guide description, it details their ethnicity, their language and reviews from previous customers.

True Story:

In Namibia, I hired a guide that spoke the language of the indigenous tribe that I visited. I was so fascinated with the culture and traditions of the Himba tribe and was so excited to be in their presence. Having a translator to communicate for me and reciprocate what the tribe was saying back to me was priceless. It was so personal and intimate, which made the experience even more special. The tribe was very appreciative that I took the time to actually talk with them instead of coming into the village and just taking videos and pictures.

1. Language Changes

As with many things culturally, languages change from country to country. And even the language of a country may not be spoken the same throughout the country. For example, a northern region's language may have different pronunciation or slang words from the same country's southern region. That's why even though you may have a great working knowledge of a language, you should hire a guide or be familiar with a local in the particular region you are traveling to.

2. Common Language Greetings

Listed below are some of the common travel words in various languages used across the globe. Again, having a guide fluent in several local dialects is an invaluable resource for your travel. Besides understanding the language, your guide will know common customs, courtesies, histories, and religious holidays of your place to explore. The last point is especially good to know when planning as far as roads, transit systems, restaurants, and tourism that may be shut down for religious events or parades. It is not necessary to try to learn a new language of a place you will only probably visit once in your lifetime, but it is good to know courtesy words. Here's a list of common courtesy words and various languages around the world.

■ Swahili Greetings

***Kila jambon a wakati wake** (*TRANSLATION: There is an opportune time for everything!) —Swahili Proverb

LANGUAGE (Swahili)	COUNTRY LANGUAGE (Bantu–East Africa)	PRONUNCIATION
Hello	Hujambo	Hu-jambo
Bye	Kwa heri	Kwah-hairy
Yes	Ndiyo	Nah-die-yo
No	Hapana	Hah-pan-ah
Thanks	Asante Sana	Ah-sahn-tee Sahn-ah
Please	Tafadhali	Tah-fahd-hahlee

Figure 11: Basic Swahili Greetings and Pronunciation. These are just a few basic Swahili greetings to get you by.

■ **Italian Greetings**

*Veni, vidi, vici (*TRANSLATION: I came, I saw, I conquered!*)*

—Julius Caesar

LANGUAGE (Italian)	COUNTRY LANGUAGE (Italiano)	PRONUNCIATION
Hi	Ciao	Chow
Bye	Ciao	Chow
Yes	Si	See
No	No	No
Thanks	Grazie	Graht-She
Please	Per Favore	Per Fah-vor-aye

Figure 12: Basic Italian Greetings and Pronunciation. Again, these are the very basic greetings to get you by. These may change slightly from region to region.

Opuwo, Namibia

■ Spanish Greetings

Las ciudades son libros que se leen con los pies
(TRANSLATION: Cities are books that you read with the feet!)
—Quintin Cabrera

LANGUAGE (Spanish)	COUNTRY LANGUAGE (Espanol)	PRONUNCIATION
Hi	Hola	Oh-Lah
Bye	Adios	Ah-Dee-Yos
Yes	Si	See
No	No	No
Thanks	Gracias	Grah-See-Yahs
Please	Por Favor	Poor-Fah-Vor

Figure 13: Basic Spanish Greetings and Pronunciation.

■ French Greetings

Rester, c'est exister, mais voyager, c'est vivre!
(TRANSLATION: To stay is to exist, but to travel is to live!)

LANGUAGE (French)	COUNTRY LANGUAGE (Francais)	PRONUNCIATION
Hello	Bonjour	Bahn-joor
Bye	Au revoir	Oh-rev-wah
Yes	Oui	Wee
No	Non	Nawn
Thanks	Merci	Marsee
Please	S'il vous plaît	See-voo-play

Figure 14: Basic French Greetings and Pronunciation. These dialects and pronunciations may change from region to region.

NOTE: Again, as with most of these languages, the region, province, or geographic location may have slight derivations of the greeting. For example, Bordeaux French is more rustic or country to say Parisian French or the big city languages.

■ Chinese Greetings 万事开头难。

Wàn shì kāi tóu nán. (TRANSLATION: The first step is the hardest.)
           —Chinese Proverb

LANGUAGE (Chinese)	COUNTRY LANGUAGE (Mandarin—Most Common)	PRONUNCIATION
Hi	你好) Nǐ hǎo	Knee-how
Bye	再见 Zàijiàn	Zay-gee-in
Yes	是的 Shì de	Shii-dah
No	不 Bù	Boo
Thanks	谢谢 Xièxiè	Shee-shee
Please	请 Qǐng	Shing

Figure 15: Basic Chinese Greetings and Pronunciation.

NOTE: It is important to realize that mainlander Mandarin and other Chinese languages may differ from rural regions. Make sure you hire a guide or make a friend who is an expert in regional dialects, customs, and cultures.

■ Japanese Greeting

七転び八起き **Nana korobi ya oki** (TRANSLATION: Fall down seven times, get up eight!)-Proverb. Never give up!

LANGUAGE (Japanese)	COUNTRY LANGUAGE (Japan)	PRONUNCIATION
Hello	こんにちは Kon'nichiwa	Koh-nee-chee-wah
Bye	さよなら Sayonara	Sigh-yoh-nah-ruh
Yes	はい Hai	Hi
No	いいえ Iie	Ee-ye
Thanks	ありがとう Arigatō	Ah-ree-gah-toh
Please	お願いします Onegaishimasu	Oh-nay-gai-she-mahs

Figure 16: Basic Japanese Greetings and Pronunciation.

NOTE: It is important to realize that Japan has many islands that make up the country. These remote villagers have remained isolated in many cases for thousands of years. A Japanese person living in a modern city like Tokyo will speak differently than a Japanese person from a rural region such as Okinawa. Make sure you hire a guide who is an expert in regional dialects, customs, and cultures.

■ Swedish Greetings

Gränserna för mitt språk är ***gränserna för min värld***.
(The limits of my language mean the limits of my world.)
—Ludwig Wittgenstein

LANGUAGE (Swedish)	COUNTRY LANGUAGE (Sweden)	PRONUNCIATION
Hello	Hallå	hahl-low-ah
Bye	Hejdå	hey-a-du-ah
Yes	Ja	Yah
No	Nej	Nay
Thanks	Tack	Tahk
Please	snälla du	snail-lah-doo

Figure 17: Basic Swedish Greetings and Pronunciation.

NOTE: As with many of the previously mentioned languages, you should hire a guide or have an expert readily available to avoid miscommunication. Many of the remote areas may not speak the same dialect as the mainlander Swedish people. Also, there may be certain cultural practices and laws for that particular province or region.

■ Thai Greetings

กว้างหนึ่งศอก ยาวหนึ่งวา หนาหนึ่งคืบ *gwaangF neungL saawkL yaaoM neungL waaM naaR neungL kheuupF* (People are the same world round; they are deserving of equal respect.)
—Thai Proverb

LANGUAGE (Thai)	COUNTRY LANGUAGE (Thailand)	PRONUNCIATION
Hello	สวัสดี S̄wạs̄dī	so-wah-dee
Bye	ลาก่อน Lā k̀xn	Lah-kahn
Yes	ใช่ Chì	Chai
No	ไม่ Mị̀	Mai
Thanks	ขอบใจ K̄hxbcı	kahk-die
Please	โปรด Pord	Puh-ord

Figure 18: Basic Thai Greetings and Pronunciation.

NOTE: It is important to realize that Thailand again is a collection of islands that make up the country. These remote villagers have remained isolated from modernity for thousands of years. A Thai person living in a modern city like Singapore will speak differently than a Thai person from a rural region such as Labuan.

Conclusion

Communication is a critical component of travel. It's helpful to understand the food signs, travel directions, and the specific law for a country you travel to. It's also a safety incentive to know what people may or may not be saying about you. This falls under staying alert as you travel. That's why my preference is to always have a tour guide when I'm out and about in a foreign country.

Beyond the language, you should definitely know all the laws, customs, cultural norms, and religion as well. Language greeting and effective communication can help some with bridging the gap.

And remember, just because English is spoken in a metropolitan or big city of a destination country, doesn't mean it's spoken everywhere. Rural, and remote communities may have never heard English spoken, much less understand what you are saying.

Follow my advice in this instance. Try to learn the basic courtesy words like 'Hello', 'Thank you', etc. Like me, you may be wanting to go to the most rural areas. Your curiosity and interest in customs and culture may be as relentless as mine. But, when visiting rural areas where English is not common, I encourage you to hire a guide that speaks the native language of the people. Do not worry about the cost, because it's usually very inexpensive (especially in third-world countries).

What will we be learning about in the next chapter? What if you need to utilize a place on a layover quickly for some reason? Where do you search for the best phone or computer app to help you on your journey? Heck, what is the best app for such a task? Let's say my train was stopped for repairs, my flight had to land unexpectedly, or my cruise ship had to be docked at a new place. Is there any way to learn about my unexpected destination?

Of course, there are! Explore on with me as I will give you great advice on some valuable resources.

CHAPTER 9:

Never Get Bored

Just to travel is rather boring, but to travel with a purpose is educational and exciting. **– Sargent Shriver**

Traveling is more than just saying that you went somewhere. Your travels should be an experience, the *Ultimate Experience* each time you land. What makes my adventures the most memorable are the things that I do, the people I meet, the food that I eat, and the knowledge I acquire. You should never get bored on a vacation, unless the purpose of your travel is to be bored. If you travel hours on hours just to relax, then maybe you should save some money and time by renting a nearby hotel, and just relax and sleep there. Abandon the thought that traveling is something you have to do just to say you did. Many people travel and absolutely hate it. They make everyone else around them miserable on the trip, and loathe their company. That's why I always say to start-off traveling light, which is somewhere in your state or country. And, if you love it... then go a further. More than anything, be careful who you travel with. A travel companion can either be a great asset or they can make you have a trip from hell.

Things that I do to stay busy while traveling are touring. Your girl loves amazing tours. I always accomplish thorough research on things to do in the place that I'm going to visit. It is never my desire to go somewhere and stay in the hotel the whole time. Every single day I have my adventures pre-planned, which helps me choose my outfits. I live for a gorgeous garb in the setting of a beautiful landscape.

Great Apps for Touring

The app I use for tours is Viator (https://www.viator.com/). What I like about Viator is that it gives you the price, description of the tour, duration from start to finish, inclusions, exclusions and the reviews from previous customers before you even purchase a tour. I usually only book a tour with companies that have multiple reviews and high ratings from tourists. That way I can read the real experiences and perspectives of previous customers. Viator has connections in almost every country in the world. All you have to do is search the city, state or country and they will provide you with the available tours in the area according to your desired date. Sounds easy, right? Well, it is just that simple.

Viator is my go to touring app, especially when I am traveling solo. Be mindful that most travel guide agencies that have listings on the app have a 2 person minimum to reserve a tour. However, some companies do accommodate solo travelers (if that is you, look at the requirement). Just take your time and look through the various tours before you finalize your booking with one. What I love about the app is that you have a cancellation period if you have a change of plans.

On my most recent trip to Asia, I came across a tour app, called Klook (can be accessed online at https://www.klook.com/en-US/). I downloaded the app to my phone because it was widely favored and used in Japan and South Korea, which were the countries I was visiting. It reminded me a lot of Viator and was convenient. The tour rates were very reasonable and very user-friendly. Klook offers things to do, places to stay (hotel recommendations), transportation, sim card and wifi, etc. It was my first trip using Klook, and definitely won't be my last.

The app I use to find private guides, which I mentioned earlier, is "Private Guide" or online at https://pg.world. All you have to do is search according to the desired country. You can even choose the preferred language. To give you an example, I searched specifically for a Himba-speaking private tour guide on the app. It was definitely needed so I could communicate properly with the Himba tribe that

Fathala Wildlife Reserve, Senegal

I visited in Namibia. Communication is very important when you are trying to connect with people. Interacting with people culturally while traveling is very important to me. Having a translator has proven time and time again to be a priceless tool to bridge that communication gap.

My Traveling Philosophy: Be the Orchestrator

Life in general includes many highs and lows, as well as ups and downs, which are inevitable. You can simply just go with the flow, or you can take control and be the orchestrator. I orchestrate my travels, and my dreams to have a more abundant life. The reason I created my travel company Mor Life is because that's what I experienced when I traveled… more life. Nothing is more discouraging than not having something in life to look forward to. Seeing how people live, both good and bad, makes me grateful for all I have. Luxury

Cartagena, Colombia

accommodations give me motivation to keep working hard, so that the luxurious life is always obtainable.

As a child growing up, travel was not an activity or privilege that I was afforded. In fact, my mother has never been out of the country. And, my father has only been out of the country a few times. So, you can say that I have, through my many amazing travels, cultivated change. My plan is to expose my children to travel early in life and support their desire to travel independently once they become an adult. I will never place limitations or cast my fears on my kids. I really want to break the generational curse of fear, doubt and closed-mindedness. Complacency with dysfunction and regularity is abolished in my life. This is an era for new possibilities and opportunities.

My first ever experience out of the country was to Stockholm, Sweden in 2008. I went there to visit my boyfriend at the time. It truly was a trip that sparked my interest to travel. He played basketball overseas in many countries, so it was always intriguing hearing his experiences in different parts of the world. He was the one responsible for exposing me to travel and I will be forever grateful to him for that. I had told myself after that one life-changing experience traveling solo to see him in Europe that once I graduated nursing school, I would travel the world… and that, I have been doing ever since.

Lake Bunyonyi, Uganda

Conclusion

There is so much to explore in the world. Yes, round of applause that you have arrived in a foreign country, but now what are you going to do? I want you to not only tour and explore, but I want you to do so safely. Only book with accredited tour companies and agents. I like Viator because they are verified and list full information. No doubt that there are probably a few faulty companies on the app, but that is why I only book with the tours that have reviews and greater than 4 star ratings.

Be the leader and the director of your life. Don't only make moves because other people are making moves. Research and learn so that you can create opportunities for yourself to explore and travel. Use the apps listed for starters. However, there are many more apps and resources to ensure that you never get bored while on a vacation aka holiday.

Now, here you are on your amazing vacation, living your best life. You look up and it is almost time to go home and you have failed to capture any moments of your experience. Is it because you were enjoying yourself just that much? Or, because you went by yourself and had no one to take a picture or video of you? Well, don't even worry about it, I have some tips to solve those minor problems in the next chapter!

CHAPTER 10:

Don't Let The Memories Fade Away

I hope to bring back pictures from the world that open people's eyes – pictures that suggest the enigmatic nature of the world we live in, as well as its variety, complexity, beauty, and pain.
— Alex Webb

Time passes on whether we are ready for it or not. Our memory, as with many things concerning time, will eventually fade. That's why now it's important to capture your *Ultimate Experience* while you can. Take pictures, keep a journal, open up a video record. For posterity, put it on a channel (YouTube or your own webpage). Maybe even write your own travel book or even a blog and share your own truth with the world.

Lompoul, Senegal

1. Camera & Pictures

My most amazing pictures come from the strangers I ask while traveling! Most people traveling have the same desire to capture the moments and they do it well. I always run into photographers that know all the bomb angles. Not to mention, your guides are experts at capturing the best picture, being that they generally do it every day. Most importantly, I recommend getting a multi-use tripod which can support a camera and your phone. There are timer apps and even timer features on popular social media apps like Instagram and Snapchat. To get even fancier, you can get a Bluetooth remote so you can take the shot from a distance. Please trust that it is very possible to capture content on your journey even when you are traveling alone.

PRO TIP:

If you are traveling alone, don't be afraid to ask someone to take your picture!!!!

■ Camera/ Picture Checklist

- ■ Pick a camera that is durable for travel.
- ■ Keep a few memory cards or cartridges depending on the camera. You will be surprised how quickly you can fill one of those up.
- ■ Identify your camera with a signature, emblem, stamp, or something that signifies that it is your camera.

- Secure the camera as you would anything valuable.
- As with any presentation, select your topic or subject to take a picture of carefully. Never take unwarranted pictures of people or prohibited objects. It's very disrespectful and rude.
- Do your research in advance to get the right idea about how you want to shoot the picture or how you want your picture to be shot. I have acquired a lot of knowledge by watching YouTube tutorials on photography and following professional photographers on social media for tips. And I must say… I've gotten damn good at capturing content.
- If possible, keep a backup camera (in case it gets lost or damaged), plenty of batteries or charging systems.

2. Keep A Journal

Pictures capture the delineation of the landscape. However, words written in a journal translate what you are feeling in the moment, what happened in a particular instance in time, and keeps you in alignment with your inner self, which can really solidify the true experience. Sure, pictures are great, but they can't convey what you were actually thinking or feeling back in time. Words written are your thoughts. Don't let the memories and thoughts fade away!

Journal Checklist

- Pick a journal that is durable for travel. Wind, weather, seas, and heat can easily destroy a journal.
- Keep a journal that has a minimum of five hundred

Chiang Mai, Thailand

pages—you will be surprised how easily and quickly you can fill one of them up.

- Identify with signature, emblem, stamp, or something that this is your journal.
- Secure the journal as you would anything valuable.
- A journal with a lock is a great idea. You don't want prying eyes knowing your thoughts unless you allow it.
- Dates, places, and time should be recorded somewhere for each journal entry.

3. Create Videos (Vlog, YouTube, or Other)

Nowadays, everything is about recognition and acknowledgment. My advice to those who want to travel is, don't do it for social media or gratification from others; find a better reason. If the only thing that you are doing your entire trip is taking pictures and videos versus taking in the beauty of the place in which you are in and enjoying yourself, you are doing it all wrong. Memories are precious, so flick it up (of course)! But just make sure you take a good look around you. Even influencers and bloggers must find a balance between participation in the excursion and documenting content. Moreover, there are many travelers who get paid to explore the world. Ultimately if you are getting paid to do so, that's a different situation; get your money! As of yet, my travel has not consisted of business, so that's out of my scope.. but I do aspire to in the near future. To date, I travel for the vibes and exploration of the countries I visit.

In celebration of my love for travel, I started my YouTube channel, called **"Morgan the Explorer,"** not for financial gain but to highlight my travel journey to inspire others to explore the world. I share my experiences, different places I have been, and what I learned during my trips. In the two years that I have been uploading videos on my YouTube channel, I have managed to develop a small and friendly community of watchers who are inspired by my travels, and it makes it worth the hassle. I use the word hassle loosely because I am the type of traveler who loves to engage in the culture, participate in activities, go on tours and taste the native foods, amongst other things. On the other hand, in vlogger mode, when I stop to capture a moment, it sometimes takes away from my personal experience. Nonetheless, I remain committed to vlogging because I want to give those who do not otherwise have the opportunity to visit for themselves the chance to see. Receiving feedback from all the viewers that have successfully traveled based on my vlogs is rewarding and makes me very happy. I have learned how to monetize my channel, so it has turned into a source of passive income, which is amazing.

Everyone always asks me what camera I use while vlogging, so of course I will share. Initially I started out using a Canon G7x Mark II. What I love about the G7x is that it's ideal for traveling because it's compact, durable, has good battery life, dynamic range, full HD video, customizable manual controls and overall, a high-performance camera. My favorite feature is that it has a

180-degree tilting flip and front-facing screen that is great for recording and taking a picture or video in selfie mode.

Much of my experience with vlogging has been trial and error. Every trip I become more advanced in capturing content. Instead of capturing every little thing, I have learned to capture things of value and the importance of clarity. Also holding a steady hand and not chewing gum (the sound can be picked up) when shooting a video, was a lesson I learned the hard way.

Nowadays, I use a DJI pocket 2. Let's just say, I love this camera so much. The best feature about it is that it's pocket-sized and extremely durable. The gimbal for stabilization is absolutely flawless, which is perfect for a steady and smooth video. The microphone is outstanding, 64MP photo, 4K video, 8x zoom for detail, noise reduction, and much more. I purchased the creator combo from Best Buy for $499.99 and it was worth every penny. If you just want the camera, it costs about $350 retail price. Hands down, the camera is a 10/10 to me.

PRO TIP:

Make sure you get insurance on your camera!!!! Of course, if you lose it, the insurance will not be useful, but it comes in handy if it gets damaged in any way. Once while on vacation I dropped and broke my DJI, and when I took it in for repairs at Best Buy, they replaced it with a brand new camera without question because it was not repairable.

■ Video Log (Vlog)/ Channel Checklist

- ■ Recording equipment should be durable and dependable.
- ■ Keep the equipment out of the elements during travel. Wind, weather, seas, and heat can easily destroy the equipment and video.
- ■ Keep a travel vlog to a maximum of fifteen minutes. You really have to tell the entire story without making it boring and too lengthy. A lot of people's attention span is short, so make it interesting in order to retain your audience. If the video is going on longer than fifteen minutes, maybe break up the videos into two to three different videos with edits depending on the total recording time.
- ■ If you find the topic or country you are covering has a lot of information, you may want to make a documentary. Keep the documentary to no more than an hour to two hours maximum. Again, you will lose your audience retention going on too long.
- ■ Have more recording cartridges or memory than you need. I usually go through at least one 128GB SD card easily while on vacation. Now I always pack a few.
- ■ Identify your camera or recording devices with a signature, emblem and stamp.
- ■ Secure the camera and recording equipment as you would any valuable.
- ■ Dates, places, and time should be recorded somewhere for each vlog or channel entry. Personally, I dislike having timestamps on the actual videos and pictures, but I transfer all data to my computer into folders in chronological order.

- As with any presentation, select your topic or subject to record carefully. Approaching a person and recording them without permission and authorization is rude and disrespectful. Please, always ask before you start shooting footage or taking pictures.
- Do your research in advance to get the right idea how you want to shoot the video.
- If you plan on capturing content on your phone to upload to YouTube, always record horizontally. If your content is going on your Instagram (reel or story), record vertically. I learned the difference the hard way. I was vlogging my entire trip vertically with the intention to upload it to YouTube. When I went to edit, I realized that the vertical format did not fit the YouTube screen ratio (16:9). Nowadays, I use my phone for social media (Instagram and Facebook) and use my DJI to vlog for YouTube.

Conclusion

To recap, time will move forward whether we are ready for it or not. There is a certainty that our memory, as with many things concerning time, will eventually fade. Take all the pictures you can and if you can't, don't be afraid to ask someone else to take the picture or video for you. Keep a five-hundred-page journal if you decide to jot down your thoughts. Open up a video recorder with tons of back up recording memory cartridges. And if you really want to have it for posterity, put it on a channel (YouTube, Rumble or your own webpage) to share with the world and most

importantly your children one day. Maybe even write your own travel book or blog…. you never know who it might reach. The sky's the limit!

So you followed the advice and took as many pictures as you could. You even went the extra mile and decided to further remember your adventures by writing a journal. And, you might have even gone on to make your own YouTube channel and travel book. What else could we possibly explore? Well, there's always more.

With all the dangers going on in the world, what mindset should you have when you go exploring? What motivates you to venture into strange remote places? Before you make your journey into our mysterious world, read on to explore my perspective and philosophy on traveling.

CHAPTER 11:

More Travel, More Life

To travel is to live. — Hans Christian Andersen

Embrace all this world has to offer when you travel. I know it's a hard thing to say these days with all that has been going on the last couple of years—wars, conflict, and illness. But I still believe in the greatness of all people. Humanity always finds a way to endure, persevere and move forward. The same can be said when we go out into the world and be amongst other cultures while making lasting memories.

Have something to look forward to in the latter years. A happy place within your heart and mind that will always give you a smile. Life is more than going to work, going home, cooking, cleaning,

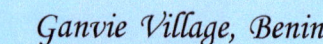
Ganvie Village, Benin

caring for the children and your spouse. Life is about learning, exploring, experiencing, laughing, love, peace and happiness, among other things. Do not limit yourself or your aspirations. Live life to its maximum extent. The more I travel, the more I am grateful for my life and value all that I have. To go further, it has awakened my understanding about other cultures, religions, customs, economies, etc. My imagination has no boundaries, as I have seen so much and know that there is even more to see.

It's okay to not be ready YET! Before I had the liberty to travel, I was on the grind doing all I could to make it to a position of contentment and freedom. When I say freedom, I am referring to the ability to make a decision and having the means to move freely to carry out that decision. I have built a life that I am proud of and have the means to move about the earth as I please. If that is your desire and goal, it will come to pass (believe it). Everyone has their own timing and should not rush to keep up with someone else. Instead, discover your purpose and walk in it with confidence and pride, knowing that you are living your life for yourself.

My perspective on having a good time was different from most. I never had a desire to be out all the time, partying and splurging my money on expensive things….. let alone, traveling if I didn't have anything to show for it. To the contrary, I started off my travel ventures as a celebratory event for each goal accomplished and milestone reached. This resulted in me always

having something to look forward to. I knew that if I kept achieving my goals, I would make more money, have more freedom and ultimately more travels coming up. It is not my belief that anyone should be out in the world stagnated and never rising up from where they are. But instead, consistently flourishing, challenging, progressing and expanding one's territory.

Life is so amazing and should be celebrated at all costs. I never want to go through life and not experience all it has to offer. From my experience, travel has opened my mind, heart and soul to things I never knew existed. I have been fortunate to learn so much history, knowledge and gain clarity through my travels, which has been so important to me.

You may know how much money you have, but you don't know how much time you have, so spend it wisely. Don't allow people to dim your light because theirs is burnt out. Instead, let your bright light be the reason they light theirs again. It should go without saying to never allow someone who's lost to give you directions. I say all that to say….. a person that has never traveled anywhere will never be able to scare me into not traveling. Growing up in South Central Los Angeles, I have been robbed of my jewelry off of my neck, my car has been stolen from in front of my house, I have been a witness to all levels of crime and violence…. so excuse me if my skin is a little bit thicker than most. Staying vigilant and aware of my surroundings is a skill I learned very early, which has kept me safe on my journeys around the world.

Conclusion

The moral of the story is to create a life that you can look back on and smile at. Yes, the pandemic has been a living nightmare for some with losing loved ones to covid. For all of us, social distance and isolation was a new experience, and for most we still somehow contracted it no matter what protocol we followed. What we have survived is a testament that we can not predict the future, all we have is now. Do not allow people to project their fears onto you. Going through life paranoid and scared is not a life you should want to live. Playing it safe, by only going from home to and from work, does not guarantee you safety. The likelihood of you getting into a car accident is 1 in 5000 vs. a plane crash is 1 in 1.2 million, so please take that into consideration.

Life is so grand, yet precious and should be handled properly. Aspire to be the best person you can be mentally, physically, emotionally, and spiritually. Everytime you accomplish something good, reward yourself… because you deserve it! Move beyond stagnation and complacency, because nothing new will come from that space. If you want to learn something new, go to new places and explore new things. Broaden your own territory and space on this earth, and that will inspire you to expand the limitations you have placed on yourself. I encourage you to live your best life… please LIVE!

CHAPTER 12:

It's Okay to Go Alone

The man who goes alone can start today; but he who travels with another must wait till that other is ready.

– Henry David Thoreau

Before I start, I want to reference a great poem that sums up my *Ultimate Experience* when I travel to all these exotic places. The words resound lyrically as epic drums beat in a euphoric song of bliss. They just seem to capture so eloquently what I'm feeling in these magical and mysterious moments. I hope it conveys to you my overall philosophy for travel and the theme of this book.

Afoot and light-hearted I take to the open road,

Healthy, free, the world before me, The long brown path

before me, leading wherever I choose.

Henceforth I ask not good-fortune, I myself am good-fortune,

Henceforth I whimper no more, postpone no more, need nothing,

Done with indoor complaints, libraries, querulous criticisms,

Strong and content I travel the open road.

The earth, which is sufficient,

I do not want the constellations any nearer,

I know they are very well where they are,

I know they suffice for those who belong to them.

–Walt Whitman

As mentioned earlier, most of my trips have been solo. The reason being is my understanding that not everyone can get up and move on my time. At this time in my life, 90% of my friends have children, which is a beautiful thing. It would be delusional for me to think that they should abandon their children to come explore with me every time I decide to get up and travel. Also, financially for most people traveling is not a priority or in their budget, and that too is okay. My comprehension that the world doesn't revolve around me gave me the courage and determination to get out in the world and see it for myself. When traveling solo, I can travel according to my convenience.

As much as I love my solo trips and freedom, hopefully in the near future, I too will become a mother. I do believe taking time off from traveling will annoy the hell out of me, but my biological clock is ticking. If I hop on the motherhood train, as soon as my child is walking, he or she will become my travel buddy! My parents never took me and my siblings on trips and vacations, so I am eager to break that cycle and share the world with my child(ren) when the time comes.

Sometimes things may come up when you plan a trip with a friend, family or spouse. Maybe its fate or maybe the stars misalign and bad luck creeps in. Never fear. Where there's a will to travel, there's a way. Go, although it may be alone.

Here's my top eight reasons why it's okay to go alone:

EIGHT REASONS TO GO ALONE (SOLO TRAVEL)

1. You will be drama free.
2. You won't have to make concessions on what you'd like to see first or where you should visit above all else.
3. You can choose when you want to leave a destination.
4. You can come and go as you please.
5. You miss blame if you make a colossal mistake.
6. There's something to be said about not hearing the snores, the stomach grumbles, or erratic breathing while on vacation.

7. You will be less likely to catch a cold or stomach ailment.
8. There will be no delays waiting for others to reach the destination if there's an incident in transit.

I'm sure you are thinking some of those reasons are outrageous, but it's truly a relief when you don't have to experience them on a trip you have been highly anticipating. Let's discuss in detail the points of each reason to explain the pros and cons for each.

1. You are drama free.

The first was not having to deal with hearing drama from family, friends, or a spouse. I mean you go on vacation to relax. The last thing you want to hear about is the troubles of others. From conversations about gossip to talks about negativity that one had to bring on the trip from home. I could go on and on about various situations about drama, but you get my drift. Nothing can ruin a peaceful sunset on a beach, a swim under a waterfall, or a fun night of dancing while someone is stirring the pot.

Now the cons of this are obvious. You run a greater danger traveling alone and not in a crowd. The people that you bring along will know you in your day-to-day back home. They somewhat are trusted and groups seem to be fairly safe in foreign countries. So, it's up for you to decide.

Wait, one more thing on the drama. If you are the type that enjoys dark gossip, can't wait for the fall of another, or just enjoy hearing or delivering pain unto others… stay the heck away from me. You really have to be mindful and intentional with who you travel with. In vacation mode, I have no tolerance for drama. I'm trying to get my *Ultimate Experience*, you hear me?

2. You won't have to make concessions on what you'd like to see first or where you should visit above all else.

You have that wonderful Hanauma Bay Beach picked out in Hawaii. You know the beach with all the caves of coral and the jagged rock cliffs? Sure, it's going to be a climb down and back up from that white coral beach. There's going to be tourists flocking later in the day. You plan with your friends to leave at seven from Oahu to beat the crowds and get an early spot. Then the whole plan comes crashing down. Your one friend planned horseback riding up in Waimea Falls. Another wanted to take the group to The Pearl Harbor Museum. Oh, wait another got the tickets to head over to Big Island for the Kona Coffee Tour. You can see the arguments brewing away until fights start kicking off. Not to mention, one is hungover from the night before and is man down bad, so they aren't even saying anything at all. Sounds like a straight vibe killer, right?

Alone you plan your day. Alone you trek to the bay and snorkel until the sun goes down watching sea turtles. Since there's no waiting or deadlines with the others you go to Big Island or whatever island you choose. Best of all if a crowd shows up, you're by yourself and don't take up much room on the beach, trailhead or wherever. It's the peacefulness for me!

The cons of this approach of course are you will be alone once again. There won't be anyone to share your experience with. There won't be safety in numbers of a group. Worst of all, if there is a mechanical breakdown of your car, plane or whatever, you'll be stuck or stranded alone. But, hey for some like myself, it would just be another adventure in a day of the life of a traveler.

3. You can choose when you want to leave a destination.

Deadlines and commitments can be a pain. You went on vacation to get away from the rat race and being chained to a clock only to be chained to the time clock of family, friends, spouse, or even worse…. a group of people you don't even know (travel group trip). You can go ahead and double the time it takes to go to and leave a place as there will always be one who lingers back or struggles to keep up. Restaurant reservations and travel by planes, boats, trains, jeeps, and even submarines if you choose, need advanced planning to get all folks there at the same time. And you can bet that someone will have an issue and be delayed.

So, you go alone and you take that cool submarine ride down along the Bahama coast and have the time of your life. You don't have to worry about someone missing the tour, you can get up with plenty of time to spare, and best of all… You won't have to wait on the rest when you are done.

The cons of course are you won't have anyone to talk to in line waiting to ride whatever. You miss out on the sharing experience and storytelling of a travel delay. Which in all honesty is overrated in my opinion.

4. You come and go as you please.

As with earlier, you plan out that special restaurant, beach, and night club. Then it all gets shut down because one of your companions gets sick, gets in trouble or worse…. jailed. Hell, what if they just blow off your idea and go alone without even telling you. The latter could be enraging of course and sad if you are the sensitive type. Then there is the problem with booking a group at certain restaurants. If you brought a village on your trip the restaurant might have a set policy of the number of patrons at a table. And we won't even go into details of where people like to sit and with whom on these group trips. Again, another chance for drama. And…you know how I feel about drama.

But you went alone on the trip and dodged the stress of coordinating groups of people to agree on the restaurant, beach, etc. You didn't have to face the irate restaurant people having to accommodate or bend their seating rules. Best yet you missed out on the ensuing arguments of who gets what chair. By yourself you make your time and you determine how long you want to stay out in a location. In a group you compromise and have to leave on a consensus.

The cons of course are you don't get to share the storytelling and laughing at the restaurant. Nor will you have someone to talk to while you scramble onto the beach or into a nightclub. And as always there is the safety of the group in remote places.

5. You miss blame if you make a colossal mistake.

Vacation and travel are supposed to be fun and relaxing times. However, tensions can flare when you travel with people and things don't go as planned. It's really important to be flexible and go with the flow for the sake of making the best of your vacation regardless of potential problems. Bookings of hotels may get mixed up or planned tours canceled, bringing disappointment and possibly anger in some cases. Long standing feuds with siblings, friends, a lover, and parents may even intensify in what was supposed to be a jovial experience. You make the mistake of mistakes and forget to book that super popular boat trip to Phi Phi Island while in Thailand and you receive the infuriating comments and unpleasant looks the remaining duration of the trip. To add insult to injury, they will remind you about that one mistake for the next thirty years back home.

But you avoid that humiliating disgrace, and go solo. You dodge the yearly chastising for the next thirty years of your social faux pas, because you did the smart thing and went alone. There won't be any fighting or screaming as no one will be there if you do make a said hypothetical mistake. And the best part, who's going to know you screwed up if no one was there to see it? You can dust yourself off and try again, like Aaliyah said.

Remember always: What happens on your adventures stays on your adventures, unless you want to share.

Now the cons are of course safety, but besides safety…. There are no other cons in regards to this topic.

6. There's something to be said not hearing the snores, the stomach grumbles, or erratic breathing of a significant other in the room.

Some folks are cursed to be noisy sleepers. And their family, loved ones and/or friends, who stay in the same room with them suffer a most horrid fate of enduring the groans, snores, and grumbles trying to rest themselves. Some people have medical conditions such as orthopnea, obstructive sleep apnea or other sleeping disorders that affect airway passage. You can imagine the diesel engine snoring as you are in the same room resting, or that horrid grumble of the stomach or worse in the midst of your own dream. And I'll skip the smell-a-vision image being awakened in the middle of the night with a family member you were forced to bunker down with unleashing a gastric odor to wake the dead.

I'm going to keep it real with you. Maybe that diesel engine is you… or even me! To get even more technical, what if our

body releases are fouler than anyone else's? Well guess what, no one has to complain about hearing or smelling anything coming from you if you go alone. BOOM!!!!!

But you skipped the flatulence today. You pushed forward by yourself and have had the best rest in years alone. You ordered your room and were blessed with a king size bed big enough….for well just you. No cheese smelling feet from your spouse, companion or whomever. No gastric unholiness from the same group in the middle of the night to bring you to retch. All pleasant, uneventful, flowery dreams alone.

Now the cons. Well, I see no real cons in this one. With the exception you'll miss the usual warmth of a companion.

7. You will be less likely to catch a cold or stomach ailment by not being exposed to a group of people all the time.

Everyone has illness on their minds these days. Especially when you travel and come in contact with so many. COVID, influenza, pneumonia, SARS, and take your pick of stomach bugs. It's a risk when you travel solo, but add one to ten or more people with you on a trip, and you are tempting the odds of getting sick with eventually catching something. Too many hands and faces touching and interacting in a remote environment then coming back to interact within the circle.

So, if isolation taught us anything over the last years it was the importance of distance. When you stay away from large groups of people, especially any number of sick people, you are more likely to stay well. I know it's counter-intuitive to the concept of travel to go out, explore and experience other cultures. But notably if you travel into an area where a community has an illness, solo is the safer bet.

The cons of course are you won't be sharing your travel experiences. Again, the cons always include safety. A group fares better in wilderness or natural environments from all sorts of predators—including man.

8. There will be no delays waiting for others to reach the destination if there's an incident in transit.

Travel is tough enough getting from one destination to the next. But add in more than one person traveling from several different travel areas, all trying to reach the destination point. Believe me, someone may most certainly run into an unexpected delay. In regard to time zones, say one traveler is leaving California and another is leaving with a three-hour time difference in New York. One of the two surely will be waiting on the other. And let's not forget about the weather that results in plane delays. I believe TSA checkpoints, immigration, schedule delays and long waiting times at the baggage carousel come into play as well. At any rate, the group has to wait on the many or few delays which usually adds to that frustration factor we mentioned earlier. So the relaxing vacation—pre planned and thought out for every contingency—has just taken an unexpected turn. It's certainly not the best of times for all. Even for the poor, delayed traveler.

But you went solo. There's no one to wait for in order to check in at the hotel. There's no headache of having to cancel or re-arrange a room if you have got a suite. The reservations to the swank restaurant or show won't have to be scrubbed due to your group not all arriving. Best yet, you can plan on an early or late night exploring the town without the whine of someone saying they wished so and so had made it in time for the festivities.

The cons here are the same as mentioned. Group safety as always when you are scrambling to explore the monuments and national parks may be at risk. And, of course you won't have that late group member to share the good times.

Do Not Let Fear Hold You Back!

The purpose of this chapter is not to persuade anyone to start traveling solo or put anyone up to the challenge. The intention is to empower those that are scared and apprehensive, but still have the burning desire to experience it for themselves. There is power in testimony and evidence of proof in front of you that it's not only possible but worth it. I have provided you with my reason why I travel solo, but I will also share some more safety tips that I exercise while on my solo trips.

Do not over plan, but instead just be organized. Patience and flexibility are what I grant myself. Going with the flow has always been a strength that has afforded me so much grace. I always start my mornings very early (between 6 and 7am), which allows me to get breakfast before the rush of tourists. Ordinarily, I am amongst the first to get out and arrive at all of the tourist spots. Following a jam packed day of adventure, I get back to my hotel in time to shower and get dressed for dinner. By the time I finish eating dinner, I am ready for bed by 9pm at the latest and sleep like a baby. Being "woke" and keeping a much needed sense of awareness, I never desire to stay out too late or club because it's too crazy nowadays. I was just in Japan and paid a tour guide to take me out to experience nightlife, and I surprisingly really enjoyed myself. If you are the type that just has to be out on the scene at night, please stay vigilant and safe.

Know your surroundings. I tend to study google maps before I even leave home. Most times if I'm taking an uber or private car, I put the address into my personal GPS on my phone to ensure the driver is going in the right direction (google maps is my go-to) …. Yes, I know it's a little compulsive, but my goal is to stay safe.

Don't be too social

Many people always advise me to be more sociable and make friends on my travel journey, but I'm always very skeptical. I really believe you need to use sound judgment and good discernment when it comes to befriending people while on your journey alone. Not everyone has the best intentions nor do they truly care about your wellbeing when just meeting you. Do not get me wrong, there are many people out in the world that have a heart of gold and have more potential to be better to you than your own family and friends…. but do not assume that for everyone you meet. Have an open heart, but also have an open mind and be on point at all times. Always trust your intuition a.k.a your gut….. nine times out of ten, it's a valid feeling.

True Story:

I was in a taxi going to my hotel. My GPS started as soon as I sat in the car. I kid you not, the driver was going in the totally opposite direction of where I requested to be taken. Immediately, I said "excuse me, where are you taking me?" He said "I'm taking you to your hotel." My response was "No you are not. You are going in the wrong damn direction. Take me to my hotel or let me out NOW" My tone made it clear that I was not f***ing around. Sure enough, he turned the car around and he took me to the correct location. Thank God for my GPS, because what if I just went with the flow. Truth be told, drivers take detours to avoid traffic, take shortcuts and increase the mileage in order to charge more. Of course, when you take an uber the GPS system is displayed but taxis and private cars do not, so always be aware.

Know your strengths and weaknesses. Understand that solo travel is not for everyone, and that is okay. Having the tolerance to travel solo does not award you a prize or make you any better than anyone else. It really just boils down to preference. Trust me, it was never my intention to become an avid solo traveler.... It really just happened because someone canceled and I still went because it was a nonrefundable trip, and I just so happened to really love it. Life is about taking chances and progressing regardless of who's moving forward with you or not, and that includes traveling if you will.

Traveling solo challenges you to expand mentally, and encourages you to grow as a person. It boosts your confidence and self-esteem. It is my belief that I am a better and more well-rounded person due to my travel experiences around the world. I have become a better problem-solver and very intuitive as a whole.

Being a nurse caring for all races and nationalities makes a huge difference when I have experienced someone's culture firsthand outside of my own. My appreciation for life and all that I have is much more profound. Having seen so much despair in so many countries that I have visited, the desire of my heart is to spread awareness about resolution which is to render relief to suffering. Above all things, the things lacking in many countries around the world are only resources and money, because I have experienced the most love in the poorest living conditions. Yes, we have much money and power in the US, but we lack empathy, love and peace. Total chaos with all the mass shootings, police brutality, racism, black on black crime, scandals, crime, etc, are all things that we have grown accustomed to which is sickening. In these times, you have to pray and really live your life to the fullest.

I will not lie and say that solo travel is free from fear and uncertainty, but I will tell you that I experience peace that surpasses my own understanding. If you decide you want to give solo travel a try, envision it. Watch vlogs to get a visual of the place you are going to visit to become familiar, then imagine yourself there. YouTube is such a great asset to the world. You can literally see any and everything on YouTube, which is why I created my channel. Generally, I decide where I want my next travel destination to be by watching a video or a reel on Instagram. I read and research a lot, but I am a very ocular person and I always conceptualize everything before I partake in it. I would say that my mind has a mind of her own, but she never fails me. I try to visualize everything pure, everything perfect, everything bliss. However, I am a realist and understand that not everything will be absolute. Nonetheless I believe that if you go into something with a positive mindset and optimism, you will have a better outcome. To date, all of my experiences have been ultimate and I wish the same for you in your future endeavors.

CHAPTER 13:

My Best Experiences

I have had the pleasure of experiencing various countries around the world, and I have enjoyed all of them in different ways. However, I have my top 10 countries that were my favorite above all others. Below are my top ten countries in order of my preference.

1. KENYA

Kenya is my favorite country in the world. It offers rich and authentic culture, and I have had the pleasure of experiencing it first-hand. I have always been intrigued with the indigenous tribes. Most importantly, it was in Kenya where I had my first interaction with autochthonous people, which were the Maasai people. I remember back in 2017, upon meeting the woman leader of the village I was visiting… She said "You are one of us," in her

Maasai Mara National Park, Kenya

The wildlife inspired awe and wonder. Abundant fauna was everywhere within the miles of vast landscapes. I stood in wonder watching warthogs waddle through mud and muck. Baboons chattered and screamed maniacally as they traversed the trees and grasslands. I observed the sway of the tall giraffe as they grazed leaves in the trees. You could hear the gallop of the antelope and zebras as they grazed the tall yellow grasses in the brilliance of the sun. And there was that ever present scent of primal things—possibly predators lurking in hillsides or watching in the scrub brush.

native language which was translated to me by my tour guide as she examined my features, height and body structure. Her conviction and surety behind her statement inspired me to do an ancestry DNA test, and guess what? The results stated that I was 13% Kenyan. So, it's safe to say, I really am one of them.

In Kenya, as I traveled, I recalled gusting winds across the plains and mountainous valleys. I was stunned by these gorgeous vistas consisting of endless plains that covered 1,510 square km (583 square miles) across Maasai Mara National Park.

Maasai Mara National Park, Kenya

In and around that beautiful national park, the level of luxury camping is insanely enchanting. On my recent trip to Kenya, I stayed at Neptune Mara which has amazing tent accommodations. The canvas tent literally had everything from a steaming shower to a stand-alone tub, a desk and lounge seating area, not to mention a firm, king size bed. There I was right in the Maasai Mara, immersed in the splendor and the incredible beauty of nature. Steps away from my tent was a river full of hippos! Their roars were loud and you could feel things shaking when they moved about in the water.

The food was impeccable and the vibe was top tier. I could never travel to Kenya without visiting a Maasai village and spending the entire day with them learning their history, traditions and modern-day customs. The last time I was there, they were so welcoming that they even taught me how to bead and make jewelry, which is one of the primary sources of income for them.

One of my bucket list adventures was to ride in a hot air balloon. But never did I think I would ride a hot air balloon in the motherland! The whole experience I felt was like a powerful, noxious, euphoric dream. I must concede the only drawback was the price. Also, you have to arrive well before the sun rises. But waking up at 3:30 am, and paying $450 was surprisingly worth it. If Kenya is not on your list of travel, it should be! To get a full visual of my experience, check out my full vlog on YouTube "Morgan the Explorer".

2. TANZANIA

My second favorite country is Tanzania. Have you ever watched the Lion King? Well, that movie was inspired by the Serengeti, which is one of largest national parks in the world (Kruger national park in South Africa is the biggest). The Serengeti is native to the famous Great Migration. It shares its borders with Maasai Mara National Park (my favorite). Indigenous tribes also reside in this country. Tanzania is Africa's visual masterpiece. It is a country of natural splendor, astounding wildlife, seductive beaches, charming ancient towns, archaeological sites, and geological wonders. Africa's highest mountain, Mount Kilimanjaro is home to Tanzania. Let us not forget that it has some of the clearest and bluest ocean water I've ever seen. In Tanzania you get the best of both worlds. The mainland and the island. Zanzibar is a small island that contains a lot of history. Intoxicatingly beautiful and alluring, Spice Island with 100-year-old giant land turtles roaming around. I stayed at a luxurious beachfront hotel and indulged in delicious cuisine. The exotic fruits were to die for. On my morning walks along the beach, I stopped and visited with the local Maasai women on the beach sitting on the sand under the palm trees, where they made beaded jewelry and waited for tourists to pass by for sales. Literally, Zanzibar was a surprise that offered everything that I could ask for in a relaxing, self-caring, solo adventure. I highly recommended Tanzania for honeymoons, couple trips and even group travel.

Zanzibar, Tanzania

To get a visual of my experience, check out my full vlog on YouTube "Morgan the Explorer".

3. Japan

My solo visit to Japan was my most recent trip…. And it was epic! I took a direct flight from LAX to Tokyo, which took a total of 12 hours to reach. I was sure to board the flight exhaustedly tired, so I could sleep the entire flight and wake up in Tokyo ready to explore. To be honest, the plane tickets and accommodations were outrageous because of peak tourism due to the cherry blossom season. However, it was worth every penny. I stayed in the city of Ginza which was right in the heart of tokyo and offered upscale shopping and dining.

The food was absolutely delicious, with an abundance of sushi, ramen, tempura and fresh seafood. Each region has its own specialty dishes, which provide a diverse flare. Japan is one of the cleanest and safest countries in the world. The country offers unique and rich culture, deeply rooted in tradition. There are many ancient temples, castles, and museums to choose from. The night life exceeded my expectations. Because I was traveling alone and wanted to experience life after dark in Tokyo, I hired a personal guide to take me out…. and we had a great time! Bottle service, good music and exceptional vibes was the theme of our night.

Technology is top notch and innovative to say the least. TeamLab is a must-see digital art museum, which features interactive and immersive art installations created by technology. Due to the popularity of TeamLab, book your tickets far in advance and don't miss out like I did. Shibuya crossing is the world's busiest pedestrian crossing and is something to be experienced if you can tolerate walking in the crowd of a few thousand people at one time. Just above the bustling walk is Shibuya sky, which has an amazing 360 degree observatory deck overlooking the entire city offering a panoramic view. Trains are the ideal form of transportation and are the most convenient, as well as affordable. Mt Fuji is a sight to see, and its snow covered tip is best visualized on a clear sunny day. I did a self-guided tour to Mt Fuji via the bullet train, but I would recommend joining in on a group tour for less hassle and more convenience. I didn't have time to visit the famous amusement parks such as Disneyland and Universal Studios, but I plan to bring my nephews and nieces and/or my own kids back when the time comes. From Tokyo, I took the train to Kyoto, where I stored my luggage in a locker at the train station and did a self-guided day tour around the city. Once evening came, I got back on the train and arrived in Osaka for the night. I stayed at the W hotel in an executive suite and took myself on a luxurious solo date night, where I indulged in a fine-dining experience at Mydo (located at the W). Everything about Japan was fascinating. Definitely on my top 10 list for sure, and I will be returning soon.

4. Peru

I felt the energy when I stepped off the plane. Peru is such a dynamic place full of magical wonders. The ancient heart of the great Inca Empire, Peru is a country with an amazing history. Located on the West Coast of South America, south of the Equator line. Just be mindful that altitude sickness in cities like Cusco is very real. Due to the city altitude of 3,399 meters/11,152 feet above sea level, 50% of travelers get AMS (altitude mountain sickness). Altitude sickness is basically caused by lower levels of oxygen, which occurs the higher up you go the thinner the air gets… resulting in less oxygen that is needed for our bodies to properly function. Don't let that discourage you from going though!

There are many remedies, such as having your doctor prescribe you Acetazolamide, stay hydrated (drink plenty of water), drinking coca tea, eating coca candy (you can find it on every corner and local store), practice proper breathing techniques, don't drink alcohol or smoke, and take it easy. Luckily, I did my research because I was ahead of the game and had my doctor give me Acetazolamide which is actually a diuretic, but is also prescribed for AMS. The medication actually made me kind of nauseous and drowsy, so I purchased coca candy, which is a natural remedy at the store and I was okay.

Peru is famously known for the archaeological wonders of this civilization, such as Machu Picchu, which is named one of the

seven wonders of the world. From Poroy station (Cusco), I took a luxury scenic train ride with panoramic windows to enhance the view. Once I arrived, and laid eyes on Machu Picchu which was built in the 15th century, I quickly understood why it was listed as a world wonder. It was literally a site to see.

Have you ever heard of Rainbow Mountain? Rainbow Mountain in Peru stunned my eyes. It had staggering colors of magenta, turquoise and emerald. Well, I hiked about 2 hours to get to the top, which looked like it was straight out of a Lucky Charms cereal box. Located 16,000 feet above sea level, the hike was moderate in difficulty, but totally worth it. Paying to take a horse ride up to the mountain is an option for people that are not physically fit or have difficulty dealing with altitude sickness (which is no joke), so please be prepared.

Peruvian culture is rich and immensely diverse in terms of geography and landscapes. I was able to engage in the culture, learn about the Peruvian history and sightsee all of the tourist hotspots. With lush tropical rainforests and the Amazonian jungles. Once I experienced Cusco, which is the most tourist city in Peru… I took a flight to Puerto Maldonado to explore the Amazon rainforest. There I stayed in an eco-friending lodge that did not have WIFI nor electricity after a certain hour. My purpose was to become one with nature and disconnect from the world around me. It was definitely a trip that I will remember for a lifetime. Peru is most certainly a country to experience.

5. Namibia

Namibia is safe, and easy to navigate through with well-developed roads and low levels of crime. It's the country where I first ate game (safari) meat, such as impala, zebra, oryx and kudu, which were all definitely unusual tasting textures of meat. Talk about being the home to some of the most fascinating tribes! Namibia is certainly a country of great people and so many wonders!

Indigenous people in Namibia make up about 8% of the total population and reside in various regions throughout the country. In the capital city Windhoek, you can see Herero women in their traditional dress in the local markets selling beaded hand-made jewelry. One of the best indigenous tribal experiences I have had was in the Himba village. I hired a private guide to drive me 8 hours north to meet the stylish and interesting tribe. I was welcomed and accepted by the chief into the village. There I spent the entire day talking to them via translation of my guide who spoke the native language, and I allowed the women to dress me head to toe in their traditional daily wardrobe. Another fascinating tribe was the San Bushmen people, who are believed to be the oldest inhabitants in Africa. They still live in the nude and practice ancient traditions. I was fortunate to spend a lot of time in the desert and learn history from my guide, who was a staff member of the hotel that I was staying at. I had the pleasure of lodging in luxury accommodations and seeing the biggest stars, seeming as if I could reach out and pick them out of the sky.

Windhoek, Namibia

Being the lover of animals that I am, of course I had my tour guide take me on a game drive at Etosha National Park. To be honest, I wasn't impressed by the amount of wildlife that I saw there (I have found East Africa to have the best safaris). Natural attractions, the Namib desert, Skeleton Coast National Park, Kalahari Desert and Damaraland, are all options for an adventurous traveler. Everything from deserts, sand dunes, diverse wildlife, dramatic scenery, local culture, and beyond. There is much to see and do in Namibia, and if you ask me…. The country is highly underrated.

Immerse yourself into a great time visually! Check out my full experience on my YouTube vlog "Morgan the Explorer".

6. Turkey

Turkey is packed with historic landmarks, outstanding architecture, museums, fine dining and diversity. They have also recently recorded the oldest civilizations in the world. A visa is required for US citizens and can be purchased online (as of now, 2023). To be honest, I purchased my visa upon arrival for 20 USD, because the online visa was a bit confusing. I flew into Istanbul (IST airport), and I stayed at the W hotel, which was right in the heart of the city. Cruises on the water with live cultural entertainment are one of the most common must-do activities during the night. I roamed around the city via taxi and on foot in most cases, and I did feel safe. However, I was very conscious of my belongings and my environment, because there are low occurrences of theft such as pickpocketing in the crowded tourist areas. There was much to do in Istanbul, which is a tourist hub.

From Istanbul, I took a short one-hour flight to the charming city of Cappadocia. Imagine witnessing dozens of hot air balloons hanging in the sky like a canvas. It's such an enchanting sight to see. In addition to breathtaking morning views, there's so much to see and so many places to go. There are various activities such as camel riding, ATV driving, museums, caves to explore, pottery classes, etc. Cappadocia felt like the city of strong romance, which sucked because I was there alone and a little jealous if I'm being completely honest with you. Definitely a place where lovers thrive. Renting a dress or a tuxedo and doing a professional photoshoot is nothing uncommon, it's really a big deal. Of course, I engaged in a photoshoot, but looking back now.... paying $700 USD was extremely too much. They have much cheaper photographers, just hashtag Cappadocia photographer on Instagram and take your pick.

Luxury hotel accommodations are definitely an option and an experience that I indulged in. The Capitol Hill hotel offers rooms formulated out of caves with a private individual built-in

Cappadocia, Turkey

heated pool and sauna, literally a dream. Definitely a place I want to return to with a love interest of mine in the future. For sure I will be visiting again. To get a visual of my experience, check out my full vlog on YouTube "Morgan the Explorer."

7. El Salvador

With just a short straight flight from my home city airport (LAX), it was a convenient travel that was budget friendly. There is so much to see, with affordable tours and activities. Gaining much popularity over the past few years now due to increased safety, it's a must visit country. I landed at the airport (SAL), had my private guide pick me up and take me directly to my hotel to get dressed. I wasted no time exploring, having him take me from the hotel straight to the famous rainbow slide which cost only five bucks. The name of the place was Picnic Steakhouse, which is a restaurant that added the slide to attract tourists, which definitely worked in their favor. The landscape of San Salvador was great and the food was amazing.

It is said that the pupusas (national dish) are to die for, but I didn't get a chance to try them. I did a lot of city-hopping at some of the most popular spots and attractions. I hiked Santa Ana Volcano, which was moderately challenging physically and took about 2 hours. The turquoise crater at the very top was a spectacular sight to see. I love a good adventure, and El Salvador didn't let me down. Exhilarating activities such as suspended bike

ziplining and surfboard ziplining, was a real treat for me. There was a natural hot spring that originated deep beneath the Santa Teresa geyser, Santa Teresa natural spa provides massages, mud baths and natural pools at your leisure. You cannot visit El Salvador and not go to Nawi Beach Club. Rather you stay at their hotel, which is Mizata or only get a day pass for $10.... It is a must. The food, drinks, music, black sand beach and infinity pool, bring all the vibes to life. I woke up at the crack of dawn and started my day with a beguiling private yoga session on the beach. El Salvador was definitely an amazing solo summer trip that I will never forget. If you want a great visual experience of El Salvador, check out my full vlog on YouTube "Morgan the Explorer".

8. Jordan

The country is affordable, yet you can still indulge in a luxury experience. If floating in the Dead Sea with a good book isn't on your list of things to experience, it should be. Just please don't shave your legs the day of, or day before (I know, hard to believe I said that!). But my freshly shaved legs were literally on fire from the high concentrations of salt in the water. A mud mask applied to your entire body is a necessity and is said to reduce skin impurities and is rich in minerals.

Jordan is home to one of the Seven wonders of the world, which is Petra. You have to see the magnificent Treasury Building, which attracts hundreds of thousands of people a year. If camping

Dead Sea, Jordan

Amman, Jordan

is your thing, Jordan is the perfect place to do it. Visit Wadi Rum, which is also known as The Valley of the Moon. Miles and miles of gorgeous desert landscape. I literally felt like I was on Mars. Staying in my luxury bubble tent with transparent walls was the highlight of my trip. I felt like the queen of glamping (luxury camping).

Regardless of proximity to other warring countries in the Middle East, Jordan is known to be the safest. I explored the country solo, and I did not feel scared at all. Going from city to city, starting from the south crossing the border by foot from Israel, I explored many popular cities. Once I reached the capital city of Amman, I stayed at the W in a luxurious suite… I felt like the rich auntie that I aspire to be.

Amman is historical and has roots back to biblical times, and is recognized as one of the oldest cities to continuously exist. The Citadel, as known as the Temple of Hercules, is an archeological site in the center of the city on the highest hill in Amman. You will never get bored in Jordan, as there are plenty of places to see and things to do.

The Jordanian people were all very friendly and welcoming. To get a visual of my experience, check out my full vlog on YouTube "Morgan the Explorer"!

9. Uganda

The country that is home to gorilla trekking, which left me in amazement. A true adrenaline rush is how I will describe it. Gorilla trekking is conducted all year around in Uganda, and neighboring countries such as Rwanda and Congo. I chose to do Gorilla trekking in Uganda specifically because it was the cheapest, although the permit cost was still a whopping $700 USD. Encountering the majestic and mysterious silverback gorillas was a time to remember. Dry mouthed and wide-eyed in childlike wonder peering into the blanketed Impenetrable Forest. The place felt so mysterious that I felt I was in a lost world. There are no words to describe the raw power of such a gentle creature. It was a once in a lifetime experience and a highly anticipated bucket list adventure that I will never forget. Trekking Chimpanzees is also an option, but that was not on my list of things to do there.

Referred to as the 'Pearl of Africa', Uganda provides culture and wildlife. Friendly people that show hospitality goes without saying. Boat rides on and ziplining across Lake Bunyonyi, made a perfect day. Hearing the wind blast through my ears as I rode a boat across Lake Bunyonyi was absolute perfection. The glaring sun wasn't too harsh and the rippling waters were so tranquil. I might have taken a nap at one point of that adventure. The winds soared through my hair, and my very eyes were filled with such terrors as I ziplined across the lake. How my arms and body ached from the activities! But it was so much fun. Bird watching

Bwindi Impenetrable National Park, Uganda

Buhoma, Uganda

is an easy task if that's what you are interested in, as Uganda has over 1000 recorded species of birds. I was able to do a game drive in the national park named after the queen herself, Queen Elizabeth National park. The national park consists of the big 5 (leopards, lions, buffalo, rhino and elephants)... however, I was a little disappointed that the park is not home to giraffes. Getting jittery and nervous like a child seeing my first lions up in the trees sleeping and lounging about when I saw them…thankfully.

Going hiking in Sipi Falls is a good outdoor activity if you are an adventure enthusiast. Having the opportunity to visit Ride 4 a Woman, which is a charity that empowers women was a highlight of my trip. Ride 4 a woman is a charitable organization to support women overcome poverty, domestic violence and HIV. More than 300 women have been taught skills such as pedal sewing, basket weaving and microfinance, in order to earn a living for themselves and their children. If you enjoy culture, the Batwa people who live in camps on the edges of the forest and still engage in their traditional way of life. Due to my short time during my stay in Uganda, I did not get to visit the Batwa community… but I plan to when I return again. Ugandan people are amongst some of the nicest people I have had the pleasure of meeting. Immerse yourself in a grand visual experience in Uganda. Check out my full experience on YouTube "Morgan the Explorer'!'

Sunset Beach, Turks and Caicos

10. Turks and Caicos

I will start by saying that Turks and Caicos are one of the most expensive countries in the Caribbean. I must warn you that a 10-minute taxi ride will cost about $40 even on a good day, but I still loved it. The level of clarity and turquoise water is a stunning sight to see. Activities such as horseback riding on the beach, swimming with domesticated stingrays, ATV riding, and water sports are all optional. If you are lucky, you can run into 'JoJo the Dolphin' who is very popular. Maybe you want to take a professional photograph from a bird's eye view in a crystal-clear kayak, which the island is famous for. The food was flavorful and the seafood was fresh.

To date, I haven't partied as hard as I partied there. Experiencing the floating bar, only accessible via boat, is a must. The yacht life in Turks is real. Known for celebrities casually lounging around the country, you never know who you will run into. That country gives 'Soft Life' vibes. To properly enjoy your vacation there, make sure you have the funds, because it costs a pretty penny to really have a good time.

CHAPTER 14:

In a Nutshell

> Twenty years from now you will be more disappointed by the things you didn't do than by the ones you did do.
> – *Mark Twain*

The truck roared through the muddy road tossing silt in its wake. Fog and water drops filled the emerald leaves in the trees as the safari truck passed them shaking off crystalline drops of rain. We were headed across a UNESCO World Heritage Site, the Bwindi Impenetrable Forest National Park, which flanks the slopes of the Munyanga falls. Once we arrived at the welcome center and were briefed about safety instructions, I was ready to do what I dreamed about doing. I, Morgan Linson, was thousands of miles away from home on a solo trip on the ancient edge of the Albertine Rift to see…gorillas! Yes, you heard that right. I was going up these mysterious mountainous trails to go on a gorilla trek! It had been one of my dreams—as I'm sure many others, to see lumbering silver back gorillas in their pristine habitat.

Petra, Jordan

Onward as we trekked through the quiet fogs of the mountains enamored by the mystery and beauty of the mountains and the long dormant volcanoes. My heart thundered in anticipation and my eyes widened while gazing up into the prehistoric landscape. I remembered as my guide led all that had been advised during our safety precaution lecture. Oh, how this 'Pearl of Africa'—Uganda gave a life experience beyond the wildest of my African Dreams!

Our hike started to become more leveled and I could feel the condensation blanketing me from the immense and towering jungle. As we came to a complete pause, there was a family of gorillas totally unbothered by our presence. I was overwhelmed with all the colors and sounds of mountainous jungle birds. Birds such as the musical Red-throated Alethe sent out their shrill calls. I was puzzled over how the Strange Weavers weaved all manner of basket nests in the trees. I shook my head in bewilderment at the Collared Apalises proudly sporting his feathers. But the incredible Purple-breasted Malachite stunned me in all its reverent plumage. So many jungle birds and so many wonderful songs that I'm still learning about to this day since that life-changing trip.

Is it your desire to travel? Then, what exactly are you waiting for!!!! Maybe your dilemma is time, money, people to accompany you, or maybe all of the above. Well, nothing is going to happen until you make it happen.

If you take nothing else from this book, I want you to remember this:

> And then there is the most dangerous risk of all — the risk of spending your life not doing what you want on the bet you can buy yourself the freedom to do it later.
>
> –Randy Komisar

And, my philosophy on travel is the second thing to remember; One thing is for sure–DEATH, and two things are for certain… LIFE is short, and TIME waits for no one. If you desire to experience the world by way of travel, I encourage you to do so at your earliest convenience. PLAN, SAVE, and EXECUTE. So many people spend their whole life working or taking care of a family, then look up one day and time has escaped them.

And as I stated before, I will not lie to you and tell you that everything involving travel is paradise, because that's not always the case. You may lose something valuable; you may run into unexpected weather changes; you may get injured or sick. However, you have to protect yourself and stay prepared. Please remember, if you allow fear to hold you back, you will miss out on mind-blowing adventures. I truly believe that lack of knowledge is the source of many, if not all, problems that are avoidable.

And here's my final reminder that I truly hope you take to heart,

> When we pass on—eventually we all must—shall our very existence drift forgotten across the immeasurable and immemorial expanse of time? I say to you, take hold and live the best memories of the world. Live the best life that you can! Fill your heart with the joys of travel, the mysteries of desire, and THE ULTIMATE EXPERIENCE of being one with our great world!

Therefore, we have come full circle in our exploring. As I reiterate my lesson to you for all your travels,

THE ULTIMATE EXPERIENCE:

1. **Plan.** Plan ahead months or even years in advance, if necessary.
2. **Save.** Again, save every penny for as long as it takes.
3. **Execute.** You put the planning and money together. It's time to get things moving.

Remember:
Every day you put off travel you miss something really amazing.

Love Valley, Turkey

Final Words

I have had the luxury of travel as a result of my hard work and dedication. It is extremely possible to work full-time and have a fulfilling travel life. To be transparent, I have had the same employer for the past 16 years, so I get vacation benefits. My advice for people in the workforce is to pick a field and job that you love. Everyday do your best, perform to your highest ability, and show up ready to get the job done. More than anything, don't just work for money, work for benefits as well. The absence of benefits is a deal breaker for me because I don't just consider the present, I take into account the future. If you are self-employed and/or a business owner, that is all the more reason to explore freely. I urge you to visualize what you want your life to look like, so that you can bring it to life. Everything begins with a vision. You can do anything you set your heart and mind to do. Traveling is an activity that you buy but it gives you back so much more.

Personally, it is the exhilaration behind travel that keeps me motivated to keep exploring the world. It has just been simply and plainly the curiosity of learning how people live in different countries that has kept me inspired to plan my travels. Driven by this approach, I have managed to travel solo across the globe. My traveling has most certainly left a mark on the kind of person I am and the kind of life I aspire to live, which is in freedom.

I know you want to ask, where will I explore next? To be honest, there's so many countries on my list that it's unpredictable where my curiosity will lead me. Most likely I will go back to East Africa and visit Seychelles or Mauritius for the first time. Maybe a return trip to Tanzania and challenging myself to conquer the climb of Mount Kilimanjaro. And, I might certainly be down for an incredible safari during the great migration. My dream vacation is to visit Antarctica, and it shall come to pass. Certainly I will give all these ideas some thought, then plan and execute, which is the rule of thumb.

There are so many places left to explore and discover! We live in such a vast, wonderful world filled with seven continents, 195 countries, and thousands of different languages, customs, and cultures. There is so much I encourage you to explore. And as you go on your own adventures, use all of the guidelines—Morgan the Explorer's visuals, pro tips, check lists, and experience on your journeys.

It is my sincerest hope that this book brings you much enlightenment, guidance and advice as you make your own way into our wonderful world. Safe travel. Wishing you the **Ultimate Experiences**!!!!

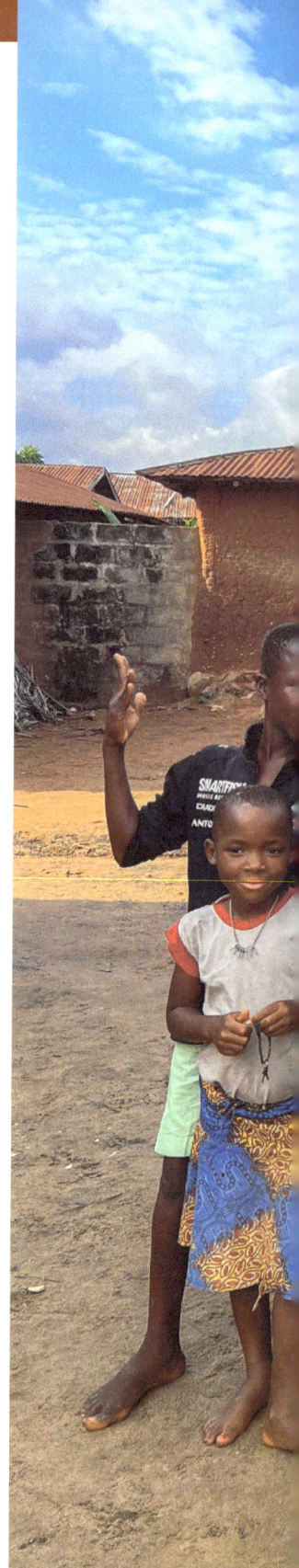

Possotome, Benin

www.ingramcontent.com/pod-product-compliance
Lightning Source LLC
Chambersburg PA
CBHW041456010526
44119CB00012B/290